Phil Donahue on . . .

HIS FIRST MARRIAGE:

"People came up to my wife and said, 'Isn't he wonderful? Do you know how lucky you are?' But I wasn't always so wonderful. There were lots of times she thought she was very unlucky. I bring as much excess baggage to a relationship as anybody."

—*Esquire*, January 30, 1979

ON FEMINISM:

"I grew up in a world where . . . all the people in power were men. Everybody in the Last Supper was a man. The Blessed Trinity was two Men and a Spirit. You can't come out of that experience without being a sexist . . ."

—*Chicago Tribune Magazine*, May 14, 1978

HIS AUDIENCE:

"I respect these women, but okay, some of what I do is showbiz. Don't forget there's a guy on the other channel giving away $25,000, and he's got a woman jumping up and down dressed like a chicken-salad sandwich, and, by God, I better have something going on my show because this is a very competitive business."

—*New York Times*, May 20, 1979

PHIL DONAHUE: A MAN FOR ALL WOMEN

Phil Donahue
A MAN FOR ALL WOMEN

AN UNAUTHORIZED BIOGRAPHY BY
JOYCE WADLER

A JOVE BOOK

Requests for permission to make copies of any part of the work should
be mailed to: Permissions, Jove Publications, Inc., 200 Madison
Avenue, New York, NY 10016

"Johnny Get Angry," lyrics by Hal David, music by Sherman Edwards
© MCMLXII by Tod Music, Inc. Arranged–Conducted–Produced by
Stan Applebaum.

Death of a Salesman, by Arthur Miller, copyright 1949 by Arthur
Miller, reprinted with the permission of the publisher, Viking Penguin,
Inc.

The Feminine Mystique, by Betty Friedan, W. W. Norton & Company,
Inc., New York, N.Y. Copyright © 1974, 1963 by Betty Friedan

First Jove edition published December 1980

10 9 8 7 6 5 4 3 2 1

Printed in the United States of America

Jove books are published by Jove Publications, Inc.,
200 Madison Avenue, New York, NY 10016

CHAPTER ONE:

Top of the Heap

> Don't let anybody tell you they don't like this
> kind of attention. Suddenly, there is money.
> Women are asking me for autographs. I go to
> lunch with Muhammad Ali. I'm enjoying it.
>
> —Phil Donahue,
> *TV Guide*, May 27, 1978

It's a hot July day and the half-a-million-dollar-a-year
man is rising. The Yugoslav couple who serve as housekeepers are already up, going about their chores in the
five-bedroom house, and one or two of the boys are
already gone on their summer jobs. Maybe only the
youngest, sixteen-year-old Jimmy, will be in the kitchen
to say good morning, or maybe not—kids are so much
more independent these days than when the half-a-million-dollar-a-year man was a boy, thirty years ago—but
then, so much has changed.

Not too much time to dawdle for the half-a-million-
dollar-a-year man. He walks from the shower, dries off,
blow-dries that mop of gray hair. Funny, he was among
the first of the Notre Dame crowd to go gray, and now
it's his trademark: was it *TV Guide* that described his
hair as "falling across his forehead like a graying snow-
drift"—a chilling image, really—and wondered how

many women, watching him on TV, yearned to run their fingers through his hair?

Or was it their feet?

Yes, that was it: "How many, while standing at their ironing boards, dreamed of running barefoot through his hair," or something like that.

That was the same story that described him as hitting daytime television "like a hormone injection directly into the carotid artery of the American housewife." There have really been a lot of magazine pieces on him lately: "Number One Talk Show Host," "Phil Donahue, Mr. Charming," stuff like that. Weird how suddenly it seems to happen that you're hot; how, when you throw a party, everybody from the mayor of Chicago to Dear Abby to Billy Carter shows; how the romance with Marlo becomes a national item. And how, all of a sudden, money is no problem at all—if he feels like treating his staff of thirteen and their spouses to a week's trip to Hawaii, well, why not? He can afford it.

No time for recollection, though, no time to dawdle. Donahue pulls on jeans and a casual shirt, heads to the kitchen to grab a bite and make his hellos, maybe play for a minute or two with Tida, the Maltese terrier, then heads to the garage for his brown Chevy Caprice—so much less bother than that Mercedes he used to drive. Men, the guests on his show often say, are much more creatures of habit than women, and you could make a case of it with him. At 8:45 A.M., at home in the suburb of Winnetka, he's usually stepping into his car; by 9:15 he's usually pulling up in front of the television studios of WGN on Chicago's North Side, wardrobe bag in hand.

So it goes this morning. The studio, as Phil arrives, is a madhouse as usual, with phones ringing, and producers Pat McMillan, Darlene Hayes, Sheri Singer—who arrive an hour earlier than Phil—making final booking arrangements, lining up guests, following leads. Thirteen staffers—not counting Phil—are crammed into one large room with boxes of videotape piled up here and there, and stacks and stacks of books all over. Pop psych, sexuality, the ever-changing war between the sexes, the newest tell-all biographies; the books flood the office, and why not? An appearance on "The Phil Donahue Show," people in the publishing business claim, can sell fifty thousand copies.

There are no authors on the show this morning, however. This morning, as it often is, it's going to be two medical experts, a psychiatrist and a urologist, and they're going to discuss a very hot subject, a subject that will probably strike a nerve in every woman in the audience: impotence. Neither will this show be two experts merely talking about the sociological or psychological reasons for impotence; the guests today will be involved in finding a surgical cure for the problem, and one will even have brought one of the implant devices for a little show-and-tell. See how *that* plays in Peoria.

Can't just sit around feeling smug till showtime, though, gotta keep moving. Donahue checks in at his small eight-by-ten office—with the pictures of Dolly Parton and his daughter Mary Rose and, of course, Marlo—skims his messages, and then—the studio audience of 200 women is already lining up outside—goes to meet his guests and, as he always does, warm them up personally.

The guests are Dr. Brantley Scott, a urologist from Houston, who has pioneered the implant work, and Dr. Paul Weisberg, from Washington, D.C.

Donahue chats with them for a few minutes, gives Weisberg, whom he has never met before, a little "Is it this hot in Washington?" stuff, and then goes over the show with them. His tone, he knows, will set the mood for his guests; if he's excited, his guests will be excited. Talking with Weisberg and Scott, now, he's enthusiastic but serious. Listening to him, Weisberg, who's never seen "The Phil Donahue Show," decides he'll be "a little straighter" on the program.

He also makes a request.

"I'd like to get one thing across, that this man is a real giant in the field, not just another Texas doctor," says Weisberg.

"No," says Donahue, "I don't want that, I don't want any sales pitches."

Energetically, he describes what he does want. He tells the two doctors that the studio audience will be predominantly women, that they will have waited two years for their tickets, and that they will be a variety of types. He tells his two guests not to feel shy about interrupting each other if they're anxious to make a point— "this is a show that needs to move fast"—and warns them that they won't have a long time to say what they have to say. "Most people feel an hour is a long time. It's not a long time," he says.

He asks the doctors to continue their discussion with him and the audience throughout the station breaks and commercials, to maintain the mood, keep the energy high, and show the women in the audience that they care. "This is the only show of its kind, and it's making it not because I'm a genius or anybody very special, but because it has audience participation," he says.

Meticulous, thorough, he asks Scott to check his surgical implant device, to see if it's working properly. (The device, only a few inches in length, consists of two cylinders, which are implanted on either side of the penis, and a round, ball-like reservoir, which is implanted as well, and contains liquid. When the cylinders are pumped up with liquid, which the man can do with a touch of his hand, the penis becomes erect.) The device, unfortunately, is clogged. Limp, malfunctioning, it's hardly a good advertisement. Concerned, Scott heads to the men's room to fill the device with water and test it out. Donahue and Weisberg follow. It's a silly scene— one of the most prominent urologists in the country bent over the bathroom sink, splashing water all over himself—and most people would make at least one off-color comment. Donahue, however, makes no remarks; to him the subject is still serious.

Donahue is no stiff, however, no robot, and both doctors—themselves expert at dealing with people—are impressed with his sensitivity and intelligence.

They also consider him a pretty good amateur psychologist; he's doing a fabulous job of motivating them, making them get excited and enthusiastic.

"I think you'll have fun, I think you'll enjoy the show," he says, over and over.

Meanwhile, as Phil is warming up the doctors, producer Pat McMillan is out with the studio audience, whipping them to a froth. "Be enthusiastic," she says, as she always does. "Speak up . . . don't pontificate, avoid long speeches . . ." She jokes and teases and goes over the subject with them. "Do you have any questions you think you'd like to ask?" she asks one group. "What are you going to do, just sit there and look pretty?"

A few minutes before air time—slightly before eleven—the long-awaited moment arrives, and Phil enters the studio from the back, alone. He teases them, speaking aloud the clichés they're thinking: "You're so much thinner in person"; "You're so gray"; he moves among them, he touches, he kisses. He also indulges in a bit of terrifically clever psychological manipulation. "Help me out, ladies," he says, "make me look good." It's an inspired technique, at once making himself less intimidating by making the audience feel more important, at the same time encouraging the members of the audience to participate—if only as a personal favor.

A moment or two later, the guests are given a glowing introduction—"As if we were the King of England," says Scott, later—and brought into the studio, to tumultuous applause.

"We were cheered as if we were prizefighters," says Scott. "Under those circumstances, you can't help but get excited."

The excitement holds. Donahue makes a serious introduction, then quickly brings the doctors into the discussion. Their remarks are graphic and down-to-earth—and obviously unsettling to the studio audience.

"You may find a man of forty or fifty getting soft once in a while," Weisberg says, "and their wives at that age—who are at the peak of their sexual activity—may become terribly angry, beginning a reign of terror at home, saying to their husband, essentially, 'You aren't giving me this, and you are wrong' . . . and it is very disturbing . . . ten million American males are impotent and there is nothing that leads a man into old age, psychologically, as quickly as impotence . . . there is nothing that closes the door as quickly to his dreams, his ambitions, his sense of self . . ."

It's a position that deals, at the moment, with the man's sense of pain, but now Phil—who has already commented sympathetically on what a painful experience impotence must be for a man—turns his attention to the woman's side of the problem.

". . . Aren't there a significant number of marriages in which the husband only looks at the wife in bed, or, after a breathless courtship in which he couldn't keep his hands off her, there's a significant change in his behavior, and a lot of women are, in effect, sleepwalking through their relationships, never having that wonderful, indefinable feeling of knowing you're thought of and cared for as an erotic being . . ."

"It's a scary thing to a man, to be intimate," one of the doctors suggests as explanation for that sort of behavior.

"It wasn't scary during the courtship," parries Donahue, quickly.

"That wasn't intimacy, it was fantasy," the doctor replies.

The show moves quickly, and in what seems to be no time at all, there's a station break. Phil jokes with his audience, walks up and down the aisles. In the glare of the bright television lights, one member of his studio audience notices that Donahue has mismatched his socks—he's wearing one black and one blue. True to his down-home image, Donahue stands up on a table and shows his mistake to the entire audience. The unspoken message is that he may be a television star, but see, he's as likely to mismatch his socks and make a fool of himself in front of a bunch of people as is your own husband, going to a party.

Donahue's attention, however, is not directed solely to his audience. He also takes a moment to quietly direct his guests. "Let's not get too anatomical," he says to Weisberg, apparently worried by a too-casual bit of language, and to both doctors, "Let's keep the answers a little shorter."

The next segment opens with Donahue soberly reminding his guests of the serious nature of the problem— and also speaking to them of all the veterans who came back seriously wounded. He also takes the opportunity to editorialize a bit about the Vietnam War.

"So after all the giggles and laughs, let's make a mental note to those men who went off to war like loyal

citizens . . . not only found themselves in a war unsup-
ported by people back home, not only viewed now as
perhaps the worst debacle in our history as a
republic . . . men in their early twenties who will never
have sex . . . it makes all the business of war, and who
decides who goes, even more painful . . ."

He moves back to the specific subject at hand.

"As a urologist," he says to Scott, "you have pioneered in the development of what has been called a
penile implant . . . and I want to see if we can sensitively
share with our viewers the nature of this device . . ."

Scott holds it up. "A man gets an erection because
of the inflation of the erectile body . . . it's a hydraulic
phenomenon," he says, as the audience looks on, thun-
derstruck. "The cylinders are placed alongside the penis
and the pump is placed underneath the abdominal mus-
cles. After intercourse, the man hits a little release valve
and allows fluid to return from the cylinders into the
reservoir . . ."

"How many implants have you done?" puts in Donahue.

"About four hundred," says Scott, thus establishing
that this is no one-shot, crackpot, experimental process.

"What's the oldest person you've ever done?" Donahue asks.

"An eighty-five-year-old," says Scott.

There's a little light banter here, then Donahue turns
to Weisberg. Earlier, Phil had refused Weisberg's request to review Scott's credentials, or praise him, on the
air. Now Donahue changes his mind; perhaps he feels
it's necessary to buoy up Scott as a serious practitioner.

"Incidentally, Dr. Weisberg, you wanted to make a
point, this is a real heavy in urology . . ." he begins.

Weisberg leaps in. "Usually, in a field, there is no
one person who is the leader . . . but Dr. Scott is the

leader in the whole field of urology in the United States, and perhaps even the world . . . there is nobody to touch him . . ."

There is scattered applause in the audience. But Donahue never allows the mood to stay fixed for very long; that way lies tedium. Now, having warmed his audience to pro-Scott feelings, he briefly turns devil's advocate.

"That's nice, take your bow," he says over the applause, then, quickly, while some people are still applauding, "Of course, some people might take your work as another example of sex as genital activity, while what we need is more personal communication . . ."

"Sexual intercourse is one of the most intimate forms of communication between men and women," replies one of the doctors. "Take that away and it has a very subtle effect on a marriage . . . it's serious business . . ."

It's time, now, for questions from the audience, and from viewers at home. Donahue leaves the stage and walks through the crowd.

His audience asks: "Have you done transsexual surgery?" "If a man is impotent, is it better for the wife to ignore it or encourage her husband to talk about it?" "My husband had a vasectomy—his first wife made him—and now he hardly ever makes love to me. Can a vasectomy make you impotent?"

Donahue stays among them, warm and encouraging, touching a woman here, taking a hand and helping a woman to her feet there.

Watching him, his guests are once again impressed.

"He's got fingertip control of his audience," the psychiatrist, Dr. Weisberg, would remark later. "He knows just who is going to ask what question and when to ask them. There was a guy in the audience who wanted to talk—looking at this guy, you could tell he was afflicted—and Donahue called on him right after the commercial break, to get up the excitement. He bestowed his smile on people when they did nicely. Simple reward/ punishment."

Meanwhile, sitting in the audience, Dr. Scott's wife is reaching similar conclusions about the host. Personally involved, as she is, with one of Donahue's guests, she has decided she should not participate in the questions, and simply refuses to open her mouth. But she also sees that Donahue has noticed her silence and is letting her *know* he knows; several times, as he walks the studio, he gives her a look that says, "Well, what's wrong with you, why aren't *you* with it?"

She is, of course, among the silent minority. All around her, women are straining to be recognized, like overeager kids in school—waiting for Donahue to call on them, help them to their feet with a helpful hand, maybe linger over them as they ask their questions.

A woman now comes on with an intriguing thought: "You mention that if a man is failing in his job, it could affect him sexually. On the other side of the coin, does that mean if you're looking for someone really sexy, find a powerful, influential man . . . ?"

Dr. Weisberg takes the question.

"A man who is a success is either the best or worst partner," he says—the maddening non-answer of a psychiatrist. "The kind of energy that goes into being a success, goes into the variety and care he takes in his lovemaking, to work to satisfy his partner and care for others. On the other hand, he could be the *worst* partner; he can be using his work for a substitute . . ."

Donahue steps in, then, with a question that seems to project some personal guilts and concerns.

"A man can also be successful on the marketplace because he's an SOB," he says.

"Well, I don't know about that . . ." says the doctor.

But Donahue is not ready to give up on this theory.

"But a lot of driving men step on people to get to be on top and I can't imagine them being very loving partners, that's my point," he says.

"Well, look at our President," says the doctor. "I imagine he would be a very loving partner . . ."

"Yes," says Donahue. "I'm not suggesting *all* successful men are that way." He pauses, turns half away from the audience, covering—but only partly—his face with his hand, in mock embarrassment. The unspoken suggestion, hanging in the air like an erotic perfume, is that *he,* after all, is a successful man, that *he's* okay in the sack. But he's too subtle and knowledgeable a performer to put that one into words. Instead, he shifts the subject of success back to the President. "I can just see the memo in the Oval Office tomorrow," he says.

The show moves briskly along. Donahue is doing well with the audience, and the bright and articulate guest, Dr. Weisberg, is doing well also. Just before he signs off, Donahue lets the viewing audience at home in on the little joke about his socks, and points out that Dr. Scott—"this big shot urologist"—has mismatched *his* socks too. It's informal, it's cozy, and as promised, it's over very quickly.

Donahue signs autographs for his guests and their children back home, not quite as energetic as he was before the show, and not—one of the doctors feels—as friendly.

He also gives Weisberg a compliment, of sorts.

"Don't ever go into television, I wouldn't want to compete with you," he says.

"I promise you, I'll never compete with you," replies Weisberg.

The doctors depart. Phil goes down to the studio again and takes part in another one of the show's rituals—

saying goodbye to every single woman in the audience.

His goodbye patter might be considered a bit paternalistic by an avowed feminist. "Go straight home, don't talk to any strange men," he teases, touching them, thanking them, giving them that famous smile.

But no one seems offended. They kiss, shake hands, tell him how much they've enjoyed the program. "God bless you," they say often.

Then it's well past noon and they're gone, and the half-a-million-dollar-a-year man has to get on with the behind-the-scenes work involved in running a hit show.

Back upstairs, it's still frantic. Requests for newspaper and magazine interviews are coming in. (*Newsday*, of Long Island, New York, gets a go-ahead; *Self* magazine, a brand-new publication, is turned down.) There are conferences with his producers for those 235 ideas his show eats up a year, and maybe a bit of criticism from them if they feel he's missed an angle or gone for the easy laugh. There will be requests for him to appear at this benefit or that, homework to do on upcoming guests. It's nice that he's finally taking a vacation next week, nice that he'll get a chance to visit with his mother, back home in Cleveland.

Cleveland. What would the sisters at Our Lady of Angels Elementary School have said if they could have seen their former altar boy with those doctors this morning, holding up that little implant? What would the brothers of St. Edward's High School have thought? And he, who was always at morning mass at Notre Dame, who was a virgin on his wedding night—if he had been able, back then, to look into a magic glass and see his future, would *he* have believed it? Would *he* have approved?

CHAPTER TWO:

A Sensitive Catholic Boy

> I grew up in a world where all the images were
> white. God was white, all the people in power
> were men. Everybody in the Last Supper was a
> man. The Blessed Trinity was two Men and a
> Spirit. You can't come out of that experience
> without being a sexist and a racist.
>
> —Phil Donahue,
> *Chicago Tribune Magazine*,
> May 14, 1978

If you want to know a man, they say, look at his father.
And Phil Donahue's father—Phil Sr., a salesman—was,
by many accounts, an outgoing and charming fellow.

"Women were always attracted to him—not in a sexual way, but they believed him," said Phil's mother,
Mrs. Katy Donahue. "He had a beautiful personality
and, in a sense, a personality like Phil's, outgoing without being loud, without being the used-car-salesman
type. He used to say he could sell all the women, but
he couldn't sell his own wife."

A good salesman, as Mrs. Donahue notes, must have
many talents: he must have the ability to impart trust;
he must not be simply a good talker, but also a good
listener; like a performer, he must be able, at a glance,

to assess his audience and give it what it wants. He must be able, say, to look at a man's worn but pressed suit, or a woman's faded but neat dress, and know that this couple cannot afford the most expensive piece of furniture in the shop—yet also know that this couple is proud. He must be able to gauge a customer's personality, to see which people are gregarious extroverts, and which customers are more subdued, to know how best to approach each, how not to offend.

A good salesman must, in short, be good with people—he must be a likable man.

Phil's father was a good salesman. "He could sell a dead rat," says Phil of his dad. But whether Phil Sr. was as content in his work as he was effective, it is hard to say, for selling was not his first trade. Before he was married, he had been a professional dancer and musician and, with his brothers (there was a whole mob of Donahue boys), had a popular band. It is possible that music was his first love.

But by the time he married, that was behind him. Oh, it had been a gay life, a happy life, making music with your family, out till all hours of the night. But there was not a lot of money in it, unless you were Tommy Dorsey. If you really wanted to make a go of it, you often had to be on the road. And even if you didn't want to tour, it meant being away from home evenings, leaving your girl at her house—or out in the audience—while you were up on the bandstand on Saturday night. No, it was no work for a young man planning a family.

So Phil Donahue became a furniture salesman, and he did well. When Phil Jr., his first child, was born in December '34, Phil Sr. had a good job, managing a furniture store in Cleveland, and Katy was—as she always would be—a housewife.

He was a big man, Phil Donahue, six feet tall, and

Katy was just a little bit of a woman, only five feet three inches. When Phil Jr. was born, since he was so large— nine pounds, nine ounces—it was assumed he would surely take after his father. But as he grew through infancy and then into a little boy, the family was no longer sure, for, while his father was a big man, Phil Jr. was a delicate child, small for his age.

"He was a big baby, but a very tiny boy, a very tiny child," his mother recalls, the fretting still in her voice after all these years.

He was also not a healthy child. As an infant, he had asthma—a terrifying thing, particularly in a baby—and though it cleared up when he was three years old, it flared up again when he was in grade school.

Asthma is a curious illness; it may stem from physical factors, it may be touched off by emotional stress. An attack may last from minutes to hours to days. It leaves its victims gasping, frightened, often with a feeling of suffocation and helplessness. It is difficult enough for adults to deal with, but it is much harder, usually, for children. For children, more than anything else, want to be like other children—to look like them, to act like them. An attack of asthma, with other children around, may be more than a discomfort to a child; it may also be a humiliating experience. The child may fear that other children will not regard him as normal; he may, himself, wonder if something is wrong with him. The experience may make him self-conscious or shy, or perhaps more sensitive to other people in distress.

And Phil had another problem in addition to asthma: he was allergic to any number of things.

"He was very sensitive to everything," his mother says. "Dampness, molds, animals, even mushrooms."

With such sensitivities, it would not have been surprising if Phil had become an apprehensive, stay-at-home child. He didn't. He was adventurous, curious, playful—and he not only did not avoid or fear animals (which could and would give him allergy attacks), he actively sought them out. And while many children, out of curiosity, out of malice, are cruel to animals—shooting frogs with BB guns, torturing cats—Phil was never like that. In fact, one of the few times Mrs. Donahue recalls seeing Phil genuinely upset was the time, in the sixth grade, that he found a stray cat and brought it back home, and was told he could not keep it.

From the time Phil had been a baby, his mother and father had kept animals out of their household; their mere presence, simply their hair on a living room chair, might make Phil's asthma flare up. Phil had always understood and accepted that. But now he balked. He refused to give up his cat. Sure enough, the asthma came back, seriously enough to keep him out of school. Mrs. Donahue still remembers, in great detail, the confrontation with her son that followed.

"He was just crying his eyes out," she says. "And I went up to his room and said, 'Phil, what is it?' And he said, 'I'll be like that—like the kitty.' I said, 'Phil, you've missed ten days of school already.' Then I went downstairs and I said to myself, 'My God, he's in the sixth grade, I've got to have more sense than him.' Finally we prevailed on some friends to give the kitty a home." Mrs. Donahue laughs, her full, frequent laugh. "You really know who your friends are when you're trying to get rid of a kitty."

It was not simply animals in distress that Phil cared about, either. He was a curious boy, curious about the world, and particularly curious about the beasts that inhabited it—even if they were merely the relatively benign beasts of the Cleveland suburbs. If it crawled, if it climbed, if it swam, if it slid across the ground on its belly, Phil Donahue simply had to capture an animal and investigate it. To this end, he sent away—by himself—for a trap that would capture wild animals painlessly. Then he enlisted the help of an older boy, the Donahues' next-door neighbor, a boy named Russell Daley, whom Phil idolized, and together the two of them would set off for the woods, with the trap and with high expectations.

The animals were never hurt, never killed and dissected. They were never shocked or frightened or teased in the name of schoolboy science. They were simply admired, gazed upon, studied.

"They'd keep them for a couple of days and nights, then take them to the valley to set them free," says Mrs. Donahue. "I can still see Phil, petting the opossum; they really look dead, you really think they're dead, you know. He enjoyed that trap so much that my husband and I bought one later on for his boys."

He was a gentle little boy. He was also a religious boy, an altar boy both in grade school and high school. These days, Phil, no longer a churchgoer, does not regard his religious background as an emotional plus. An admittedly ambitious and driven man, with terribly high standards for himself and others, he seems to feel, currently, that the Catholic Church gave himself and other Catholics tremendous feelings of inadequacy and guilt, as well as a debilitating feeling of never being quite good enough.

"Life beats us up so much," he once told a television reporter. "We worry if our breasts are too small or too big, or if our shoulders are not broad enough. Or you come home and your parents tell you you are a big pain to raise. Then you add to that Catholic theology: Life is a vale of tears you will not get through without failing, but God will pick you up anyway.

"A seven-year-old kid can believe that he will stay in hell everlasting for something he did wrong. We believed that. We carried it with us. We were so busy trying to avoid sin that we could never make friends with women, never share ideas, never care how they felt. Women were occasions of sin, the church taught us that.

"When you get right down to it, more war has been inflicted on people in the name of the Prince of Peace than for any other reason."

But if war was inflicted on Donahue by the Catholic Church, he was not dragged screaming to the front lines. His parents were regular churchgoers, but, his mother claimed, religion was never forced on her son.

"We never came down hard on religion," she says. "We felt you set yourself as an example and teach them to love their religion. We never said, 'You gotta go to church.' And they just grew up and liked going to church."

She also says that, if anything, she and her husband discouraged Phil's plans to be an altar boy.

"My husband had been an altar boy, and he said, 'Oh, you gotta be there at six o'clock,' and so on . . . and we had a tendency to shelter him, because of the asthma."

Still, whether or not something is seemingly forced on a child, most children want to please their parents—and the expectations placed on the oldest child, and an only son, can be rather powerful.

And if Phil's parents did not order him to church on Sundays, they did send him to Catholic schools, for both grade school and high school, where he learned that he had best—for the future of his holy soul—attend church every Sunday. For Catholic schools, unlike their more liberal counterparts today, were very strict in Phil's day: It was the time when Catholic girls might be forbidden to wear patent leather shoes to school, because the shoes might reflect up their skirts; it was the time when a nun (unenlightened about the terribly destructive effects of guilt) might call a naughty grade school boy before the class, tell him and everyone else how bad he'd been, and add that she, however, would take his punishment for him—and then slap *herself* smartly on the hand several times. It was a time when Confession was a fearsome event; a teenage boy had to concern himself not only with unclean acts (necking with a steady girl counted among these), but with unclean thoughts.

It was a world, says Donahue, in which he and his schoolmates were "given whole lectures on French kissing, that's how specific it got," wherein he was taught that sexual intimacy, even between couples who were engaged, was a mortal sin; wherein it was considered common knowledge that babies who died without having been baptized went to 'limbo,' a world in the afterlife that was perceived to be between heaven and hell.

Donahue was a boy who wanted to please, a boy to whom it was terribly important to be good. He tried to follow the rules the Church laid down. But, judging from the way he talks about it today, it was a strain and a burden. He also seems to feel resentful that the rules he followed so seriously are these days often disregarded.

Once he angrily told a priest, Father Andrew Greeley, on his show: "We have millions and millions of Catholics who grew up in the period which dotted the *i*'s and crossed the *t*'s and told us what was a sin, and was absolutely certain what was a sin, and did everything but present slides to us. And now comes the seventies, and all these liberals running around saying, 'You don't believe *that* stuff, do you?' and all these millions of people who labored under the stress and strain of honestly trying to live under the idealism to the letter of the law . . . It seems to me the avant garde has abandoned the loyal

Catholics who not only obeyed all those laws, or tried to, but who also built schools at a time of depression, which we can't seem to maintain in a time of prosperity . . . If I was a sixty-five-year-old Catholic, I'd be mad as hell . . ."

It was an achingly autobiographical statement, and the pain was audible in Donahue's voice as he made it. It was an acknowledgment that sacrifice and struggle made at an early age simply might not have mattered—might have been a waste of time. It seems to suggest, also, that Phil spent a terribly burdensome, difficult childhood.

Yet, if Phil's childhood was painful to him—if he suffered inside—it was not visible to the people around him. In grade school, his friends and family remember him as a happy, well-adjusted kid. He had friends, he did well in school, he was neither too shy nor too much the clown. He did not need to let the air out of his teachers' tires or put sugar in their gas tanks for attention; he did not have to do pratfalls or make silly sounds.

"Not a cut-up in school, not a fighter, just a heck of a nice guy," recalls a boyhood friend, Kevin McIntyre, who still lives in Cleveland.

His mother, not surprisingly, concurs with Kevin's opinion of her son.

"I never really saw him unhappy. He did have his little puppy-love romances—I remember that—which gave him a fuller life, but if something happened, he was able to come home and talk about it; oh, yes, he could talk to me about it—" she laughs— "Phil was *always* very talkative."

If he was talkative, of course, it might have been because he was brought up in a loving household where he was encouraged to talk, where he saw that his feelings mattered. Mrs. Donahue, as can be seen from the way she behaved when Phil brought home the stray cat, was not the sort of person who would simply issue an order or make a demand; the feelings of her children mattered. If her son had lost his heart to a stray animal, and was in tears over its future, she would not simply throw the animal out, she would acknowledge that her son's feelings were important. She was also not unduly possessive. "We always encouraged them (her two children, Phil and his sister) to have their own friends," she says, again and again. Independent of spirit herself (it was not for nothing that her husband joked that he could sell all the women, but couldn't sell his wife), she would raise independent children who were not afraid to speak their minds. She may also have had a strong influence on the sort of women her son would find attractive—for the two adult loves of his life were bright and outspoken, just like Mom.

As for Phil's father, though he was less involved in household matters than Phil would someday be ("He was a wonderful man, but he never *would* change a diaper," says Mrs. Donahue of Phil Sr.), Phil's father also took a caring role in Phil's life. A wonderful dancer from the days when he had been a professional musician, Phil Sr., in his evenings at home, taught his son to dance. Oh, he never wanted the boy to do it professionally—in fact, according to Phil's mother, he actively discouraged his son from a career in show business. ("You never could have gotten married on a musician's salary in those days, and working nights . . . he didn't think it would be the most helpful life," explains Phil's mother.) But Phil Sr. did know the pleasures of being an accomplished dancer, the delight of being able to select any girl in the dance hall and know you could lead her onto the floor without fear of feeling ridiculous or stepping all over her shoes—of knowing, in fact, that you could dazzle her. And he thought it would be useful to pass that information on to his son.

"A boy who can approach a girl and dance well, I think that gives him self-confidence," says Mrs. Donahue.

Phil did not resist. Naturally well-coordinated, he enjoyed dancing and took to it easily. (Years later, his college friends would remember, he'd get up and do a soft-shoe when the crowd went out for pizza and beer.) In fact, he liked it so well that he took dancing lessons outside his home; for quite a few years, from fourth grade till junior high, he studied tap and ballet.

His classmates at Our Lady of Angels parochial school teased him a bit about this—name one group of ten-year-old boys who cannot resist calling one of their own group a sissy when he goes off with his black tights to his ballet class—and even his mother couldn't resist razzing him a little about it. But he enjoyed his dance lessons, and he could put up with the teasing.

"You're teasing me about my ballet, Ma, but every time I go out for a team, the coach says, 'Hey, kid, you must have studied ballet,'" he told his mother.

It was a comfortable time, Phil's growing-up years in Cleveland. The war had brought prosperity to this industrial town, and if Phil's parents' generation had been through the Depression, Phil's own coming of age would be in a confident, optimistic time, a smug time, even. Cars were bigger—the bigger the better—America was all-powerful, even under the threat of Russia. It was also a stable time; the women's movement, the divisiveness within the Church, the doubts concerning America's role in the world, would not come for twenty years. And when Donahue says everyone in his world, growing up, was white, and everyone in power was a man, that's pretty much so; he lived in the west side of

Cleveland in a neighborhood that was strongly Irish-Catholic. His crowd of male friends, when he became a teenager, went to one of two Catholic schools: St. Ignatius, Cleveland's most prestigious Catholic school, old and established, and run by the Jesuits; or St. Edwards, run by the religious order called the Brothers of the Holy Cross—the same order that ran Notre Dame. The girls in the crowd attended St. Augustine's or St. Joseph's.

Phil, when the time came for him to go to high school, went to St. Ignatius. It was brand-new the year Phil entered, so that, as one of his classmates pointed out, those in Phil's class were always the seniors. The school consisted, at first, of three ordinary houses. The first year Phil attended St. Ignatius, there were ninety students and three teachers: Brother John, who, in addition to teaching, was the athletic coach; Brother Paul, who served as bandleader; and Brother Regius, a Frenchman, who ran the laboratory, and one day delighted the student body by nearly blowing up the basement.

It was not, however, a school of outrageous hijinks. Students talked back to teachers at their own risk; the dress code required students to wear ties; and for punishment, the enterprising priests sent their students to the site of the new school building, where construction was under way, and ordered them to dig a lot of dirt.

If Phil had been a fairly good little boy in grade school, by high school, his questioning mind—or his need for attention—started getting him in some trouble.

"I was a wiseguy," he once told *People* magazine. "I was always talking and the brothers knocked me around. They threw books. They slapped me. I never cried. The closest you'd come to tears wouldn't be from the pain of being slugged in front of thirty guys, but from the humiliation."

For all that, his friends do not remember him as a

troublemaker. (Maybe he was quiet, compared to others.) Phil studied, he did well, he did not fight with the other boys, he didn't hold class office—an old classmate jokes that only the sons of the funeral directors, who had the big cars, got to do that. But he had a lot of friends and he was a very well-liked boy.

He was also a good-looking kid—blue-eyed, broad-shouldered. In his high school pictures, he looks a few years older than his gawky, self-conscious classmates, and a lot more sophisticated.

Confident, too. Mr. Cool—that was the look the young Phil Donahue affected in most shots. Maybe he was trying for James Dean; he didn't wear the slicked-back DA haircut, but there was still that same slightly bored look, the eyes slightly out of focus, the partial pout. He was not shy, no way. He seems, in fact, in those early pictures, to be a boy who enjoyed having his picture taken, a boy experimenting with images the way a man or a woman (or a performer) will try out expressions in front of the mirror. Or maybe he was simply a tad more serious than the rest of his crowd. In the group pictures in his yearbook, as the boys around him grin foolishly, he looks sober, almost brooding; in his official high school photograph it's the same serious pose.

As for his high school pastimes, they mostly involved the performing arts. His heroes, in those days, were athletic heroes, much like any other kid's: Joe DiMaggio, Lou Boudreau, Ted Williams. But he was too small, too skinny, to make the varsity teams his senior year, so he contented himself (was his father pleased or displeased?) with the stage. He was a member of the high school band (first chair clarinet), an activity that required him to get to school an hour early for practice, and stay after school as well. He was a member of the high school drama club, capturing leading roles in school plays; he was also on the staff of his high school yearbook.

His was not a crowd, however, where you had to be an athletic hero to be a big man in the high school hall—or do well with girls.

And Phil did tremendously well with girls. Maybe it was the fact that he grew up with a sister, though she was five years younger. Maybe it had to do with his happy relationship with his mother. Maybe his father had been right, and it had a lot to do with his dancing skills.

Whatever, he was smooth. Where other boys his age might blush, stutter, and stumble, he could always make conversation, make a girl laugh; when other boys were clustering for safety in small groups at the side of the dance floor, he was walking purposefully across the room, approaching a pretty girl.

"He was a ladies' man," laughs George O'Donnell, Phil's lifetime friend, who has known him since second grade. "He always dated, and at a time when the rest of the guys were self-conscious, he was out on the floor dancing."

Comfortable with women as he might have been, on some levels he was also something of a puritan—and also, as he admits today, a male chauvinist.

He liked pretty girls—his mother would later take a certain amount of pride in the fact that he had always gone with such attractive girls—but the first time he saw his younger sister in a low-cut dress, he was shocked.

As for his teenage relationships with women, though most of his friends insist they weren't as bad as he makes them out to be, he *was* the stuff the feminist movement loathes: he reportedly did do all the talking on dates, and he did expect his date to do what he wanted her to do.

But if the feminists might not be crazy about his behavior as a teenager, the mothers of Cleveland daughters thought he was great.

"I think my parents always felt Phil was a safe date,"

recalls Phil's steady girlfriend from high school, Mrs. Kathleen Richards. "He had you home at the proper time, he did the proper thing—" she takes a moment or two and laughs— "and how can I say this? You didn't have to worry about him trying anything."

"I die when I see his show now," continues Mrs. Richards, whose maiden name was Kathleen Corrigan. "I'm just amazed at what comes out of his mouth. He was the most conservative person I ever dated. I wasn't allowed to smoke in front of him, and heaven forbid I ever had a drink. We used to go out to the Columbia Ballroom—that was a big place, live band, you used to get dressed up to go—and I used to sneak down to the ladies' room to have a cigarette, and then he could smell it on me."

His steady date through his senior year, Kathleen agrees with Phil's contention that he was a sexist— though no better or worse than most of the boys she knew at the time.

"The woman was definitely subservient," she says. "Not that Phil wasn't fun. He was lots of fun, I have fond memories of him . . . he was always a gentleman, he made you feel like you were someone special, he didn't ignore you when he took you out. You were his date. I laughed a lot when I was with him, and I love to laugh. And he was a hand-holder. But he *was* conservative. He was never the loudmouth at a party, and he expected the same from you . . . I'm sure he frowned on any woman going into a bar unescorted, not that he ever said it . . . and also, you could never argue with him; he was very set in his ways, so I just didn't argue. Also, you never got a choice on a date. I don't remember him ever saying, 'What would *you* like to do?' But then, those were the times, too . . ."

Those *were* the times. And, as he had done with the

Catholic Church, Phil followed the rules, never dreaming that what he had thought to be good behavior, would years later be construed as bad.

Opening the door for a girl? That was the respectful thing to do, a compliment, an acknowledgment of her femininity, the fragile flower. Taking her home? Again, being protective, being gallant. *Ordering* her not to smoke? Well, that was looking out for her best interests, wasn't it? And anyway, it was manly for a fellow to let a girl know how to behave; the girls themselves were supposed to crave that sort of macho behavior. There was even a popular song in those days, by a wispy-voiced girl singer, imploring her namby-pamby boyfriend to stop letting her push him around. "Johnny get angry," the song goes, "Johnny get mad/Give me the biggest lecture I ever had/I want a brave man/I want a caveman/Johnny show me that you care, really care, for me."

Phil, telling his date how to behave, was just following the accepted code. And it wasn't like he was an overbearing monster; he was, as Kathleen said, fun—an active, happy boy. He enjoyed dancing, he enjoyed skating, he loved to go to football games. They double-dated with Phil's good friends, Marilyn Hogan and Bill Marquard; they spent time at Phil's house; and in the tradition of parochial school students, they spent a very special night—Christmas Eve—at Midnight Mass together.

Still, says Kathleen, they were never serious, never discussed marriage. And though they saw each other steadily, it was with the knowledge that it would only be for that year, because the next year, Phil would be off to college.

A lot of boys from St. Ed's would not be going off to college. But in Phil's family, it was assumed that he would go. He was bright and obviously deserving, his parents felt. And they also wanted more for him than they had had—for neither one of them was college-educated.

The college he would attend was, his mother claimed, Phil's choice. Still, as he looked through college brochures and talked to his high school advisor, it was inevitable that Notre Dame be mentioned. The reasons were two: Notre Dame had an extremely strong alumni association in the Cleveland area; also, St. Edwards had been started by the Holy Cross Brothers not only as a much-needed additional Catholic high school, but to also serve as a sort of prep school for Notre Dame.

Phil considered Notre Dame, but wavered. He was impressed with the school, but not certain he would enjoy it.

"I think it would be a good place to have graduated from, but not to go to," his mother remembers him saying.

Still, somewhere along the line, he changed his mind. Perhaps someone from the alumni association had made a good impression; perhaps he had decided Notre Dame would be the best place for him, even if it might not seem as much fun as other schools.

Maybe, once again, he was motivated by what may have been a powerful force in him: the desire to do the right thing.

CHAPTER THREE:

Notre Dame—Studies, Theater, and Dating

The time Phil was happiest? I would say it probably had to do with the theater up at Notre Dame, taking curtain calls. We did *Death of a Salesman* once, and got tremendous audience reaction... backstage he was happy and excited as I can remember seeing him.

> —George O'Donnell,
> Phil's college roommate

A seventeen-year-old kid chooses a school for a lot of reasons: it may be out of a sense of tradition, because a father or grandfather went there; it may be out of a sense of obligation, because father and grandfather would *like* to have gone there; it may be because the school is located in the heart of a seductive and delicious city like New York or Chicago; it may be because the school is academically prestigious; it may be because it is known, as students know these things, as a fabulous party school.

Whatever Phil's reason for selecting Notre Dame, they were certainly not this last; if ever a school was the antithesis of a party school, it was Notre Dame. In 1953, when Phil entered it, it was light-years away from the permissive, progressive schools of its day.

Situated on the northern edge of South Bend, Indiana, it was a Catholic school, an expensive school (about $2500 at the time Phil attended), and a very strict school—"The West Point of the Midwest," some called it.

At other schools, students might sign out of the dorms for weekends, and even on school nights; at other schools, boys might sneak girls into their rooms, but not at Notre Dame. At Notre Dame, there were rules, and rules were taken seriously—and they were rules more serious than many young men had faced in their lives.

Freshmen, for instance, were allowed only one late night—and that was only till midnight—during the school week. They were given another on Saturday. Women were allowed in the dorms only on Sunday (of course they signed in formally, and of course the doors to the boys' rooms remained open). Notre Dame students were expected to look like upstanding, responsible Catholic men; jackets and ties were required in the dining halls.

Religion, not surprisingly, was strongly stressed. Morning mass was not precisely mandatory, but it was strongly encouraged. Three times a week, there was a morning room check (sometimes as early as 6:45!), and that check coincided with the time that morning mass was offered in the chapel. It did not just happen that way, as the priests themselves admit.

"We did everything to encourage them to go to mass on weekdays, short of a hook," laughs Father Glen Borman, a priest who was at Notre Dame during Phil's time. Father Borman does not mention encouraging the students to go to mass on Sundays—*that* was assumed. For this was a school where most of the boys had come from religious homes, and most had attended Catholic schools.

It was a religious institution. During exam time, when students always panic, students at Notre Dame took to their outdoor chapel, a placed called "The Grotto," and lit candles and prayed. ("In exam time," laughs Father Borman, "it was ablaze.")

No, Notre Dame was in no way a liberal institution, in no way one of those newfangled, liberal Eastern institutions that took the radical view that seventeen- and eighteen-year-olds were mature enough to run their own lives, make their own rules, set up their own study programs.

At Notre Dame, for example, when they had lights-out (at eleven P.M., for lower classmen!), they meant it literally. The lights in each dormitory were controlled by a switch in the office of the dormitory rector, who, usually at five minutes before the hour, dimmed the lights for a moment or two in warning, then, on the hour, simply shut them off. It was, for the undergraduates, a terribly maddening process; a student could be on the last page of a detective story (well, a guy's got to relax once in a while), in the middle of an important conversation, or cramming for a final—and then, all of a sudden, his room is dark, and whether he likes it or not, he's got to go to sleep. The university is, in effect, putting him to bed. Frustrated, students often sought to outwit the system by creating alternate light sources: Coleman lamps, candles, exotic battery-powered lamps. But many were bothered by the psychological aspects of this mandatory lights-out; it was, many felt, a controlling thing to do. Notre Dame officials readily admitted it was controlling, but they felt it was necessary.

"It was a kind of standing in place of the parents, to help the student adjust," says Father Borman.

Phil did not need surrogate parenting. A hard-working student with a strong sense of discipline, he was likely to push himself harder than any teacher would push him, and some of the Notre Dame regulations, according to friends, got a bit on his nerves. There had been rules in his home, but there had also been a sense of freedom, a sense that he had the brains to take care of himself. Here it sometimes seemed different.

As for the religious part, that was no problem; Phil served as an altar boy, and went frequently to mass. His doubts about the Catholic Church had not yet come; in the autumn of his freshman year, with dozens of other Notre Dame students, he participated in a religious retreat in Kentucky, at a Trappist monastery.

The dating part? Ah, well, that was somewhat tamer than high school. For one thing, a heavy social life was not encouraged for freshmen. For another, the ratio of men to women on the Notre Dame campus could discourage even a boy who had been as popular, back home, as Phil. About a thousand girls from St. Mary's took classes at Notre Dame, but with 6,000 Notre Dame men, a student had to be pretty pursuasive—and very confident.

That didn't really seem to disturb Phil, however. With George O'Donnell as his roommate, he settled down and pursued his studies, and began getting used to the routine of morning checks and lights-out, of a world inhabited mostly by nice, hard-working Catholic boys.

He adjusted, he adapted. And even if Notre Dame was a strict school, Notre Dame guys were anything but a docile bunch. They may not have been protesting a war or taking over buildings, as would college students of the next decade, but they were still very big on pranks. The woman whom Phil would meet and marry in college still recalls shaving-cream fights, and his roommate George talks of the time when a friend in the dorm was away for the weekend and George and Phil shredded up piles of newspapers and stuffed them through the transom into the friend's room. Phil would roughhouse and carry on and play with the best of them; as a freshman, he was involved in a water fight that so damaged his dormitory that he was called before the master of his hall the following year, and told that such behavior—if it continued—would jeopardize his future at Notre Dame.

Nonetheless, certain pranks continued. When, in Phil's sophomore year, Notre Dame officials banned Thanksgiving recess to encourage a more academic atmosphere, Phil's crowd was among the two hundred students who gathered in front of the cafeteria for a gigantic snowball fight. (Just before someone aimed the first snowball, there was a last-minute delay while some priests walked across the dividing line. One priest, after passing, playfully thumbed his nose at the crowd. They equally playfully covered him with snowballs, but at that, a security guard came after the crowd. They were *very* strict at Notre Dame.)

Phil's crowd was big on touch football (to make the varsity team at a school like Notre Dame, you had to be of professional caliber; Paul Hornung was in Donahue's class), and it was also a beer drinking bunch.

"It was a very macho crowd, drinking and swearing a lot and throwing beer around," says one Notre Dame grad of Donahue's set. "They were all very deeply into athletics, and any guy who came close to exhibiting effeminacy was taboo."

A Notre Dame grad who was a close friend of Phil's recalls one night when he inadvertently broke the code of correct male behavior.

"We went out one night, Phil's senior year, and he ordered a beer and I ordered a Manhattan. And, my God in heaven, you'd think I'd put on a dress. He said, 'Put it away,' I'll *buy* you a beer, and he was terribly serious.

In subsequent years, he even referred to it."

All this, the hijinks, the beer drinking, the high-spir-
ited athletic camaraderie, paints a picture of Phil,
throughout college, as a happy man. But reports as to
whether Phil was truly happy his first two years in
college are mixed.

Phil's roommate George, the man Donahue was closest to throughout school, insists that Phil, in college, as
in most of his life, was "outgoing and happy and very
friendly."

But Father Borman, who was the rector of Phil's
dormitory his sophomore year, remembers Phil, in his
first year or two at school, as someone whose outgoing
nature was a mask.

"While there was a certain bravado, underneath there
was an insecurity, a lack of self-confidence," he says.
Other students, among them Kenneth Woodward, remember Phil as "rather short-tempered," "grumpy," "the
exact opposite of how he appears on television," and
also "a very moody guy."

"Moody." Talk to Phil's college friends, and that
word will come up over and over again.

One of Phil's college friends—a man who has known
him throughout the past twenty years—and who today
calls Phil "a very moral, very decent human being," still
recalls him as moody, and claims he still is, to this day.

"You can be right in the middle of a conversation
with Phil, and all of a sudden he'll disappear, go into
this period of deep introspection . . . it's almost as if he
isn't in the state, let alone the room," he says.

Phil's friend recalls one such time during their college
years. It was the summer of 1955, between Phil's sophomore and junior years, and he and Phil took a drive
through the countryside, taking with them a very pretty
coed.

"A lovely girl with Irish freckles . . . Mary something or other," he says. "Phil was rather interested in her. We were going home, I was driving, the girl was sitting between us, and suddenly Phil dropped into one of his moods. So Mary and I had a conversation—nothing I can really even remember. Anyway, we took her home, Phil walked her to the door, and the next morning, Phil walked into my room—just like that—and said, 'You can have her.' I said, 'Phil, I have no idea what you're talking about.' He said, 'No, it's obvious you and Mary have a special relationship, you were really communicating, you and she are meant for each other.' I said, 'Phil, I have no interest in Mary,' but it didn't make a dent. He had made up his mind. He had his vulnerabilities, I guess."

What prompted that outburst is hard to say—especially because, after the hard grind of his first year at school, Phil had dated so often that his roommate George threatened to rent out his room. But "vulnerabilities" seems a clue; perhaps Phil, intense and serious as he was, feeling the pressures of being an only son on whom his father's dreams and expectations rested, could simply not deal with the idea of failure or rejection. Perhaps, rather than wait for Mary to stop seeing him or indicate that she wasn't interested anymore, he chose to be in control by first dropping her.

In any case, several college friends would recall his mood swings and intensity. And there would be something else that would strike them as a bit odd about Phil's college years: while he was majoring in business (he would graduate with a BBA in Commerce), he seemed to enjoy literature and creative courses more than his business major.

"He was good in English, especially writing, but I think things like accounting and finance were kind of a drag to him," says his old roommate George.

Then why was he majoring in business?

"I think because it was expected of him," says George. "His family was sending him to college, and he was very appreciative. He often talked of wanting to someday pay his father back . . ."

Phil loved his parents and respected their advice. But when it came to choosing a profession, he would make up his own mind. By the end of his sophomore year, Phil was taking more and more communications and theater courses. He also became interested in radio and TV, and landed his first radio job—at WNDU-TV, a commercial station owned by Notre Dame. It paid a dollar an hour, and Phil did mostly production work—things like setting up microphones and weather maps, and maybe, once in a while, doing a station break. Still, when he landed the job, he was so excited that he ran to a friend.

"Listen to this: 'WNDU-TV, South Bend.'" Then, lowering his voice a note: "'WNDU-TV, South Bend.'"

He also became interested in the university theater. While Notre Dame might not have been known to have a theater program like that of Bennington or UCLA, it was serious stuff: Father Harvey, the man who was to direct Phil in all his college theater work, had worked as a professional actor and had taken his degree at Catholic University under noted theater critic Walter Kerr. A typical theater production at Notre Dame might take six to eight weeks of rehearsal, twenty-five hours a week. "I was tough," says Father Harvey.

But Phil, Father Harvey adds, did not mind working.

"He took direction very well, he was very humble, he was willing to work," he says. "He was anxious to put in as much time as it would take, he was willing to do any small part. He was *not* a prima donna."

Phil had small parts in two musicals at Notre Dame: in the chorus of *Finian's Rainbow,* and as a black in the musical version of Booth Tarkington's *Seventeen*. Still, while he had what Father Harvey considered "good stage presence," he was not musical-comedy material.

"He could carry a tune," says Father Harvey diplomatically, "but he didn't have a great singing voice."

Phil did have strength, however, as a dramatic actor. His junior year, in a stiff competition against a dozen other students, he won a leading role in *The Caine Mutiny Court-Martial*.

"He took to it very naturally," says Harvey.

The school press would disagree. *Caine Mutiny* as a whole received favorable reviews in *The Scholastic,* the school's literary magazine, but Phil Donahue was one of two actors in the play who were singled out for their dreadful performances.

"Philip Donahue, as Lt. Steven Maryk (the alleged mutineer), does not invoke the slightest sympathy in the audience, he simply plays the role of a well-meaning clod who is totally unbelievable as the leader of a mutiny," said the reviewer. "Thus, he loses all the subtle naivete that the role demands, and substitutes for it a pouting schoolboy who knows practically nothing except how to swear effectively at his attorney, Lt. Barney Greenwald . . . Greenwald, as portrayed by Allen Riley, is unfortunately just as unreal as Maryk. In these two roles, the play falls far short of the mark . . ."

A review like that can devastate an actor. But Phil was lucky in a way—the *Scholastic* review would not appear for nearly a month after the play was performed, and the local press would not agree that he had been dreadful.

And on the evening when the play was performed, he was, friends say, feeling kind of high on himself—

that delicious glow the performer feels when the tension of getting ready to go onstage has left him and the excitement remains, the pleasure of being admired by strangers as well as friends. Phil had, as well, two close friends to share his happiness that evening: George O'Donnell and Jim Cooney, both of whom had been in the production. He also had, after the relative feeling of anonymity that a large college can bring, the old high school feeling of being a star.

They say that when a person is feeling good about himself, it's easy for everyone else to feel good about him; psychologists agree that sexually attractive people are often found to be those people who project self-confidence. And any actor will tell you that the adoration he receives from strange women after a performance far exceeds any adoration he's ever received from a woman he's only just met at a cocktail party—the stage does hold a certain romance.

Perhaps that all combines to explain why, at a party following the performance of *The Caine Mutiny Court-Martial*, a young woman fell in love with Phil—and he fell in love with her, also. Perhaps that's not so, and if he hadn't been on the stage and she in the audience, they would ultimately have come together anyway. Certainly it was inevitable that they meet.

The girl was Marge Cooney, the younger sister of a friend of Phil's. Visiting Notre Dame for the first time that night, Marge, who was two years younger than Phil, was tall, slender, and dark-haired—a girl so pretty that, years after that party, friends of Phil's still speak of her admiringly.

Like Phil, Marge came from a close-knit and religious family. Like Phil, she was a product of Catholic schools. Like Phil, she had been, reportedly, a rather "conservative" girl.

The mutual attraction was immediate. Marge and Phil saw each other all that weekend, double-dating with her brother. There was no question, to Phil's friends, that this was just another of his frequent flirtations.

"The sparks were just there," says George.

They dated steadily. As his involvement with both Marge and the theater deepened, Phil seemed to become a happier man. Senior year was perhaps his most fulfilling on campus, a lighthearted, relaxed time.

The football season that year was disastrous, with Notre Dame winning two and losing eight (their most humiliating moment was losing 40–0 to Oklahoma), but Phil's classmate Paul Hornung won the Heisman Trophy and there was a feeling of renewed school pride and contentment—the feeling, once again, that Notre Dame men were a very select and special brand of men indeed. There was a class trip to Annapolis and, that being a political year, there were campus visits by political hopefuls Richard Nixon and Adlai Stevenson. There was a visit by Louis Armstrong and one by Miss Sweden, and another by a young, fast-rising Massachusetts senator called Jack Kennedy, who would be awarded Notre Dame's Patriot of the Year award. (A big Notre Dame favorite, Kennedy had already been awarded a Doctor of Law degree from the school five years earlier, and held twelve such degrees from schools around the country.) There was, in the middle of the year—perhaps in anticipation of June weddings—the annual Marriage Institute symposium for seniors, with ever-paternal Notre Dame advising its students on their personal lives and very, very strongly urging them to wed. (The son of a happily married couple, and a man who would be a notorious homebody, the virginal Phil Donahue needed little encouragement on the subject of marriage. At least nine hundred seniors, however, would attend and listen earnestly to discussions on courtship and marriage, sticking around afterward to buy how-to books.)

Senior year would also be a year of personal triumph for Phil, giving him one of the happiest moments in his life. That moment of happiness would occur onstage, in a role which, as some of Phil's friends felt, had special significance to him.

The play was Arthur Miller's *Death of a Salesman*, the story of failed salesman Willy Loman, whose hopes rest on his eldest son Biff, a man who is unable to fulfill his father's dreams of success, a man who dreams of a life outside the world of business.

In the Notre Dame production, Phil played Biff, and his roommate George played Willy Loman. And, although in real life Phil's father was not a failure, nor was Phil, there were similarities: Phil's father was a salesman; he did adore Phil; he did dream that his son would have a better life than his own; and he did, with his hopes for his only son, make him feel the burden of parental expectations.

"That play might have had some meaning for Phil," speculates a friend who was assistant stage manager for the show. "The story of a traveling salesman and of his son, on whom the sun rose and set, but who never quite made a name for himself . . . not that Phil never made a name for himself; his life exceeded his parents' fondest expectations, but he always had the Biff Loman need to succeed. I think he empathized with Biff Loman that success and recognition are very sweet, and that he decided he was not going to fall into the same trap that Biff had; he was indeed going to be able to produce and perform."

Phil was also to display Biff Loman's desire to be his own man and follow his own path, rather than pursue the life his father feels is best for him, a life in business.

Early in *Death of a Salesman*—in fact, in a speech to his younger brother—Phil, as Biff, might have echoed his own feelings about the business world.

> I spent six or seven years after high school trying to work myself up. Shipping clerk, salesman, business of one kind or another. And it's a measly manner of existence. To get on that subway on the hot mornings in summer. To devote your whole life to keeping stock, or making phone calls, or selling or buying. To suffer fifty weeks of the year for the sake of a two-week vacation, when all you really desire is to be outdoors, with your shirt off. And always to have to get ahead of the next fella. And still—that's how you build a future.

The performance of *Death of a Salesman*, at Washington Hall, was a smash. The notices the next day, in the local South Bend papers, were raves, and when *The Scholastic* came out this time, it contained a rave also. *Death of a Salesman* was said to be "perhaps the best play attempted on the Washington Hall stage . . . no amount of description can justify the beauty and force that crossed into the audience."

As for Donahue's performance: "During the last few scenes of the first act, when the other son Biff, played by Phil Donahue, discovers that his father has contemplated suicide, the production begins on an upswing which does not subside until minutes before the final curtain. At this time, Donahue displays a brilliant talent and sensitivity, which he carries through, along with fine interpretation, to the end. During his last scene, with Willy, Donahue reaches the height of dramatic success as he breaks down in his father's arms . . ."

It was a glorious review. But the audience response, that evening, was also stunning—Phil took curtain call after curtain call.

CHAPTER FOUR:

Scuffling, First Job, First Marriage, First Baby

> I thought they (the broadcasting industry) would be very fortunate to be getting me. There I was, this Notre Dame graduate with big-league experience in Cleveland.
>
> —Phil Donahue,
> *Broadcasting Magazine*, July 23, 1979

College graduation, and life was golden for Phil. He had a summer job lined up with a radio station back home in Cleveland, and he was talking marriage to a beautiful girl from a good Catholic family. There had been a certain amount of sacrifice by his family to put him through college but, unlike Biff, he was not going to disappoint. In his college graduation picture, he seems to be a man with the world in his pocket—standing in cap and gown, he has one arm around his sister, and one around his mother—a model of confidence, warmth, and perhaps a bit of masculine protectiveness as well. Mother and sister wear hat and gloves; Phil's father, in tie and suit, is to the side, smiling, but a bit more restrained in his physical expression of affection than Phil. It's a happy picture, a college graduation picture from the 1950's, filled with high expectations.

Still, why not? For the Notre Dame grad—of whom there were 1,240 the year Phil graduated—the world was a happy and hopeful place.

"There were no great causes—no Vietnam, no civil rights," recalls Phil's roommate George, a bit nostalgically. "Korea was over with, which had been the main concern. We were all very nonpolitical. It was all very tranquil."

They were, in a way, a rather conservative group, the class of '57, accepting the existing power structures of Church and country. Out of the class of '57, about one in five would graduate a commissioned officer in the Armed Forces. The weekend of their college graduation would be celebrated with a solemn pontifical mass. After that mass, an American flag would be blessed and presented to the school; patriotism was far from dead at Notre Dame.

Phil was part and parcel of that group, still religious, still a firm believer in the American dream.

But there had been a serious change as he moved through Notre Dame; though he would complete his degree in business, he now knew for certain that his future was in broadcasting.

His first job, at KYW-AM Radio/TV in Cleveland, was nothing grand. A 50,000-watt station in the old NBC building at 9th Street and Superior in downtown Cleveland, the radio featured upbeat music, and Phil's role there was strictly fill-in. He wrote the news, he handled station breaks, but he also—though he was only at the station a few months—made a powerful impression on everyone who came into contact with him.

"He was a hard-working young fellow," says Sanford Markey, the man who was news director and Phil's boss at the time. "He didn't wait for a story to come in to him. And for a young man, his questions were extremely perceptive."

He was also about the most ambitious young man they'd seen around the station in a long time. On his breaks, he'd often leave the office and travel to other stations to do auditions. He sent tapes of his voice everywhere, and when he applied for work, it was for a job behind a microphone or in front of a camera—no more behind-the-scenes work for him. Broadcasting made him feel alive, made his adrenaline flow, as business studies simply never had. Never shy, always good with people and with words, Phil was in heaven on the air, knowing his voice was going to the homes of people he never even knew.

Broadcasting, to Phil—unlike business—was not drudge work; it was something he loved doing, something, as the people close to him felt, that he *had* to do.

"Phil needs the spotlight," a longtime friend insists. "I think he's a rather unhappy person, so moody . . . he can drop out of a conversation in a room full of people, be withdrawn and absolutely down . . . but give him the spotlight and he's the life of the party."

The spotlight, in this case anyway, was temporary. The Cleveland job was over as soon as the regular staffers came back from vacation, and no one was much impressed with the tapes that this nobody called Phil Donahue was mailing out.

And as much as he loved the business, there was something else, friends say, on Phil's mind: Marge, whose home was in Albuquerque. Sure, Phil had dated a lot of women; he'd always been a popular guy. Sure, he'd had a high school steady. But in college, as his roommate George had said, there had been no one special.

"He was just kinda like a butterfly going from flower to flower," says George, laughing.

Then there was Marge, and she was always on his mind—that dark hair, that slim body, that quick mind.

That slim body . . . "We all got married while having hot pants," Phil once remarked to a reporter, and Marge *was* a very attractive girl.

Phil would like to have had that one great job before getting married; he had come from a household where the man was expected to take care of the family. ("My husband was a real male chauvinist, he felt *he* had to be the breadwinner," says Mrs. Katy Donahue.) But Phil was also wearying of carrying on a long-distance romance. With the Cleveland winter on his heels, he packed up his audition tapes and headed to New Mexico, to claim his bride and take the broadcasting world by storm.

The wedding, held on February 1, 1959, was large, romantic, and traditional. George O'Donnell was the best man; the bride was attended by her father and mother and her two proud brothers, John and Jim. As for Marge and Phil, friends report that they were both a bit nervous, but perhaps with cause—both were virgins when they married.

The most noticeable absence at the marriage was that of Phil's parents. One report has it that they did not attend because they were opposed to Phil's marrying so young. Phil's mother, however, adamantly denies that.

"We didn't come because of the distance," she insists. "We had nothing against the girl or Phil. And when Marge had her first two babies, I went to be with them and help out—because I lived closer to her than her mother did. We liked Marge; we had met her at Phil's graduation . . . she was a soft-spoken, well-mannered, very attractive girl."

The wedding reception was for over one hundred people—the bride's father was a lawyer, and he splurged a bit for his only daughter. The honeymoon, a trip out West to California, was more modest; Phil had yet to land that one wonderful dream job. But Marge wasn't worried; she was, by all reports, madly in love with Phil.

The trip was leisurely and happy. In California, Phil and Marge went to dinner with an old Notre Dame classmate or two, then slowly returned to Albuquerque. The employment he found was not glorious; he became a bank teller in the Albuquerque National Bank, and, say friends, always made a botch of things. He could not sort, he could not count; his heart was not in it. He also found work at KDEF Radio—"Albuquerque's high fidelity station"—as a part-time disc jockey, but that didn't work out either. After a month or two there, he was, as he puts it, "gently fired."

Firings and hirings are, however, taken more lightly in the field of broadcasting than in the staid world of business and finance. A disc jockey may be fired because he doesn't fit the mood of a new format, or because the ratings are low, or because the new station manager has decided to make a clean sweep—it's all part of the game. Donahue knew this, although he couldn't help feeling a bit discouraged. But he kept sending out those tapes.

When summer came, he returned to KYW in Cleveland, to fill in once again for vacationers. He even tried his hand as a teller in the City Bank of Cleveland.

It was beginning to look as if he might end up in business whether he liked it or not. Then Phil's luck suddenly changed. He got word that little WABJ Radio in Adrian, Michigan, needed a news director.

Thrilled, he and Marge threw their few possessions in the car and took off.

It was not like pulling into NBC in Chicago. Adrian, Michigan, was not a very large town when Phil and Marge arrived (there were maybe twenty thousand people), and not a terribly exciting town either (it was known primarily as a retirement town for farmers). Radio WABJ

itself, a middle-of-the-road station, was just a little thou-
sand-watter. Neither was Adrian a very exciting news
town; the regular news events, coming out of the sheriff's office, were car accidents, occasional shootings
(mostly hunting accidents), and an infrequent assault.

Still, it was a genuine, full-time news job, even if it
only paid a hundred a week, and Phil was delighted. He
and Marge rented a little place on McKenzie Street, in
a pretty residential neighborhood, and Phil set about
learning the news business with tremendous intensity.

For an aspiring reporter, that meant one regular stop:
the sheriff's office. Adrian was the county seat of Len-
awee County, and Phil checked in every day. He was,
recalls Dick Germond, who was the deputy sheriff at the
time, "very personable," "happy-go-lucky." But he was
also so intense that he was an easy target for the jokes
the sheriff and his people loved to play on reporters:
planting false items in the police logs; sending reporters
off to cover elaborate murders that never occurred; de-
vising wild-goose chases.

But there was one wild ride, one day, that was not
a hoax. Phil was at the sheriff's office that day, lounging
around, talking, when word came over the radio of a car
accident—a very serious one. The sheriff grabbed his
hat and raced for his car. Phil, always eager, ran after
him. Siren screaming, Germond and Phil raced 120 miles
to the scene of the crash.

There's a thrill to being a news reporter that is very
close to terror—it's the excitement and tension of trying
to get to the scene first; the anxiety of trying to make
a deadline; the ever-constant fear, even as you're getting
wonderful material from a source, that the reporter from
a competing station, out there across the way, is learning
even more.

There is also a terror that is very close to what a

soldier feels: the fear of what you will find as you speed toward a bloody accident; the worry that perhaps you will panic or become sick at the sight of a mutilated body; the fear that, like a soldier, you will behave badly out on the field.

Phil, speeding across the Michigan highways with Sheriff Germond, probably knew those tensions. He knew that, as fast as they were going, another reporter might also be speeding to the scene; he knew that what they were rushing toward could be hideous—Germond had warned him that it wounded like a major crack-up.

But when they finally arrived at the scene, he didn't waver—he leaped out of the patrol car even faster than the sheriff.

"He was real eager and jumped out of the patrol car into the ditch, landed four or five feet from a body," says Germond. "Scared the wits out of him. He went out of that ditch in the same fashion he went into it—that fast—like turning the movie projector backward. He didn't go to any more scenes of accidents after that—at least with me."

It was reportedly a horrifying experience for Donahue. He had been to a funeral now and then, but he had never really seen a body in that condition. But if it made him approach the scene of an accident a bit more cautiously in his professional life, in no way did it slow him down.

If a story broke, it didn't matter where he was or what he was doing, or whether he was on his own time or company time; he simply dropped everything and pursued it.

Two friends of the Donahues from Adrian, Richard and Dot Boff, remember such a time. Richard Boff was a friend of Phil's from college, who had coincidentally settled in Adrian after school. Dot and Marge, through the two men, had become close friends. They socialized often and attended church together. On the eve of what would be Phil and Marge's first Christmas in Adrian, the two couples arranged to attend midnight mass together. It was, Dot Boff remembers, a joyful time. Marge was pregnant, well into her sixth month, rosy and happy; Phil was charged up about his job, learning, growing, continuously turned on. And Christmas Eve promised to be special; after mass, Phil and Marge were going to Richard and Dot's house for breakfast. But Phil never made it. As the service got under way, the fire sirens went off. There was a blaze at a local drugstore. Phil simply dashed. It would be three o'clock on Christmas day before he returned—for Christmas dinner with Richard and Dot and their families.

If Marge was disappointed, she didn't show it. She wasn't one, friends often said, to show an outward display of emotion. But one thing, even in such a private person, was evident: Marge was tremendously in love with Phil. "Marge didn't think," said one of Marge's friends at the time, "that Phil could do anything wrong. She thought the sun set and rose on him."

And all evidence indicated that Phil was in love with her. In a business where both men and women often cultivated a tough-guy image, where the talk is often fast and dirty, Phil stood out. He never told an off-color joke. He never used a four-letter word. He took no apparent sexual interest in his female co-workers. His attitude toward women was respectful, almost courtly. And when he became a father, he was ecstatic.

The time came earlier than expected, when Marge was only in her seventh month. Phil and Marge were out playing cards with their friends Winston and Jan Hoehner, who lived only a block away. It was midnight by the time they finally returned home, and less than an hour after they returned, Marge began having her pains. Phil was frantic. "Call Jan, she's had two, she'll know what to do," he kept saying, but Marge had a different idea. "No," she said, "I think you just better take me to the hospital."

Their son Michael, premature but healthy (he would be an incubator baby), was born at four that morning, and at five, Phil, too excited to sleep, was back at the Hoehner's house, banging on the door. He was a comical sight—coat open, hair disheveled, no overshoes, even though there was snow on the ground and it was the middle of an ice storm. But he was too giddy to be aware of what he looked like. As the astonished Jan opened the door, Phil grabbed her in his arms. "We have a baby boy, we have a baby boy," he kept saying.

The Hoehners were old hands at the childbirth business, but Phil, Jan remembers, "couldn't stop babbling" about it. As Jan fixed him breakfast, he described, in clinical detail and medical language, Marge's labor, the delivery, his first glimpse of the baby. When Jan finally insisted that he get some rest, he took a nap on the Hoehner's couch, then went to work at his usual noon shift—where, once again, he fell asleep.

His co-workers were touched and amused. The manager of the station, however, was unimpressed.

"God," he said. "He thinks he's the only man who ever had a kid."

A town of retired farmers, a town with only two or three industries, offers only so much challenge, and within a year, Phil was ready to move on.

Opportunity was not long in coming. A few months after he made up his mind to leave, Phil was offered a job in his home state, at WHIO radio and television in

Dayton. One sticky summer day in 1959, Phil and Marge packed up their U-Haul and set out, apprehensive but excited, as their friends Dot and Richard Boff waved goodbye from the driveway.

Like WAVJ, WHIO radio was musically conservative: Mantovani and Guy Lombardo were frequently heard. Like WAVJ, it was a small station where there were few specialties—where, in fact, radio and TV shared a common newsroom. Long hours were a professional hazard, and Phil, as a junior member of the team, faced an especially difficult shift; he began at five in the morning, as morning announcer for WHIO-AM, doing that until ten, then, for the rest of the day, he went out with a camera crew to report and do interviews for television.

He was not, he feels today, the best announcer. But he was, people noted quickly, an excellent reporter. He was tireless, he was meticulous, he had a knack for sensing a trend and looking ahead to see the coming story. Those days, the early sixties, were the days of freedom rides—and "reverse" freedom rides, in which cities in the Deep South sent black families up North. One such group in New Orleans had selected Dayton as the target area. At Phil's urging, he and cameraman Andy Cassells set off for New Orleans to do an advance piece—long before the competition.

When a mine explosion occurred in West Virginia, Phil and Andy—once again at Phil's prompting—went out on the story, covering it five days before the arrival of the national press. The West Virginia night, Andy remembers, was cold, and Phil wrapped the one blanket they had around the camera so it would run when they needed it.

Phil also had a quality every editor wants in a reporter—he refused to take no for an answer when he wanted a story, and he was tremendously persuasive.

"He could," Andy says admiringly, "sell iceboxes to Eskimos."

Phil says of himself, not immodestly, "I began to get the reputation of a guy who wasn't afraid to go out and interview Hitler, if he could find him."

He was tireless, fearless, unafraid of being considered a pest. On a trip to Canada, for a program on U.S.-Canadian relations, he pestered the government public relations man for two days to get an interview with Prime Minister Lester Pearson; an interview which, when it was finally achieved, was a tremendous coup for a small station.

And he often talked his way into places where no other reporters were allowed, coming back with dramatic, exciting footage.

One such news story began unremarkably enough: it was the anniversary of the Wright Brothers' first flight, and General Elwood P. Quesada, chairman of the FAA, was in town, to participate in a wreath-laying ceremony. Phil, prior to the general's speech, was to do an interview. The assignment held no promise of excitement—it would be, everyone assumed, a standard bureaucratic speech, heavy on self-congratulation and optimism—but Phil did his thirty minutes, and then, with cameraman Cassells, accompanied the general back to his hotel, to cover his address.

As they arrived, however, the General received an emergency call: two airliners had just collided over New York City, in the nation's worst air disaster. Even as the general was receiving the news, bodies were floating in the Verrazzano Narrows.

And—to make the story even more important—one of the planes, en route to New York, had stopped in Dayton; half a dozen local people had been killed in the crash. The general would have to go to New York as soon as possible.

Phil, of course, wanted to accompany the general, who, at the time, flew his own plane. Stunned by the crash, the general wavered. He first agreed, then refused, and went into his scheduled speech. Donahue and Cassells covered the speech, as assigned, and Phil made another request to accompany the general—and was again refused.

The general headed out to the airport, and Phil and Andy followed. As the man climbed into his plane, Phil, following him, made one more attempt; he gave the general the "thumbs-up" sign. Exhausted, the general impulsively gave in and opened the door. Donahue and Cassells ran inside, leaving the engine on their station car still running, shouting to bystanders to shut it off.

They arrived in New York with forty dollars between them, and had to hitch to the crash scene. Phil's abilities with women must have worked even then; they were picked up by a woman who had just done her grocery shopping, and on the way, Phil ate all her cookies.

At the crash scene in Brooklyn, police had cordoned off the area, and Phil and Andy had no local credentials— only those from Dayton—but Phil still managed to talk his way across police lines.

His stature at the station grew.

His popularity, however, did not.

As respected as Phil was as a journalist, he was not universally well liked in the newsroom. His intensity, his preoccupation with getting the story, often made him insensitive to his co-workers. There were shouting matches in the halls, between Phil and the disc jockeys, and between Phil and the news management.

"I don't think it was ever an intentional thing of Phil's to be rude or cruel or overimposing," said Winston Hoehner, now WHIO's news director, who was a disc jockey at the time, "but when Phil was working, his thoughts were strictly on what he was doing. He would come running into the studio with a tape to be put on, run to the engineers, didn't ask what they were doing, or if they were busy. He was just interested in the tape; they felt he was imposing on them."

But some saw it differently. "In our station, I'd say the relationship Donahue had with most people was brittle," says one co-worker. "If you weren't of value, he wasn't interested in you; if you were, he'd put on the little-boy charm."

If he was expending energy on his job, many of the people with whom he worked felt he was not expending it on getting along with his co-workers. Perhaps, as Winston Hoehner suggests, that was Phil's preoccupation with his job; perhaps it was some of the old moodiness that his friends had noticed in college. (The highs and lows of a creative person can often be rather dramatic.) Whatever, Phil was not one to keep his feelings to himself; he had a feisty and independent nature, as well as a temper—a pugnacious streak, which, at least once at WHIO, nearly got him fired.

A confrontation developed between Phil and Lou Emm, the station's program director. Phil was Lou's morning newsman at the time, responsible for doing newscasts every morning, and, says Lou, Phil was invariably late.

"We'd go on the air at 7:30, and Phil wouldn't even be in the studio—and no *way* can anyone have breath control, doing a broadcast, after running down a hallway," says Emm. "It got to the point where one day I'd finally had it, and I threatened to fire him. He challenged me to go ahead and do it, and get another newsman."

Why didn't Emm fire Phil?

"I thought about it," admits Emm, "but I thought he had young children, he really did a good job—he was a good reporter—and all in all, it seemed like a pretty poor reason to fire somebody."

Emm admired Phil's strength as a news reporter. But four years into the job, in 1963, Phil got a crack at a job that would show where his real talents were—as an interviewer. He was not the first choice for that job—however, in a way, he inherited it by default.

His vehicle for success was "Conversation Piece," a talk show with a predominantly female audience, that aired following the noon news, from one o'clock to 2:30. The show was structured to allow the listening audience to call in and talk with the host and his guests, but it was doing poorly, and in an attempt to beef up the ratings, the WHIO management started experimenting with hosts. They tried one of their disc jockeys, but found him a bit bland; Lou Emm himself worked on it for a bit, then someone thought of Donahue.

Within weeks, the ratings started to inch up. And within months, Donahue would bag a guest who would make the ratings soar.

The moment came with the assassination of President Kennedy. Using his instinct for what listeners want to know—and his persuasive powers—Donahue put through a call to the mother of Lee Harvey Oswald, and convinced her to come on the show.

The program caused a sensation, and from there, Donahue pushed for more national stories, and for bigger names. He snared Bobby Kennedy, who was then attorney-general of the United States, and Bob Hope—en route to Vietnam—four Christmases in a row. He sought the sensational, booking guests like Dr. Rubin, author of *Everything You Always Wanted to Know About Sex*, and the author of *The Sensuous Woman*. He had medical experts, often gynecologists and obstetricians and leaders in child care, so that co-workers began to say they always knew what was going on at the Donahue's house—whether, for instance, Marge was expecting again—by the nature of Donahue's guest. He was as temperamentally independent as usual; on one show, whose subject was sex education, he had booked a doctor and his wife, who was a nurse. In the course of that conversation, the nurse used a famous four-letter word, rarely heard in polite Dayton society and never on the air. Some people at the station felt she had used the word because she had been partly encouraged to by Phil, who had, during the interview, himself slipped into slang.

Phil, at that time, had an announcer's delay button, and could have bleeped out the word. He chose not to, however.

The subsequent battle with the station management was fiery.

Phil insisted the station was trying to censor him; management, in the fierce verbal battle, took the position that *they* had a license to lose, and he did not. Succinct threats were exchanged. So concerned about the tape was the station management that they held onto it—it's at the station to this day.

Ultimately, however, the furor did not hurt WHIO. And it certainly did not hurt Phil. All over town, people were starting to talk about him. He was starting to be somebody very important. He was on his way.

CHAPTER FIVE:

Clouds on the Home Front

> I don't think I got into 130 markets by being lazy.
> I think I'm Exhibit A of guys who knocked them-
> selves out in the fifties and had very little left to
> give their marriage."
>
> —Phil Donahue,
> Detroit *News*, February 12, 1978

If things were hopping at the station, and if Phil Donahue's name was beginning to be known around Dayton,
life was also not exactly subdued at home. Phil and
Marge had always wanted a large family, and Marge was
busy producing one. A second son, Kevin, was born
December 9, 1959 (the same year as their first son), and
two more sons, Daniel and James, followed at two-year
intervals. The Donahue home seemed at times like a
nursery; at one point, Marge and Phil had three children
in diapers at the same time; and children, as any parent
knows, subscribe to the domino theory of behavior: if
one screams, the others can't help joining in.

It was a madhouse.

Phil, these days, insists he was an uninvolved father
nearly every time the subject of his marriage comes up.
"In the early sixties, I still thought marriage was all apple

pie and babies, that all Mom had to do was get breakfast, send Dad to work and the kids to school, and head down to the laundry with a song on her lips," he says.

And: "Men are raised with tunnel vision—namely to go out and get promoted at work—and none of us have been prepared for marriage and fatherhood. I'm staggered when I think of how ignorant I was when I got married. Nobody told me that the kids were going to occasionally make me angry, or how important it was that they have a sense of caring for their father."

Yet this image of himself as absentee father was not the whole truth, and may simply be part of Phil's penchant for blaming himself when things go wrong. (People with high standards are usually hardest on themselves.)

It's true that Phil was at the office a lot. It's true, as he noticed from time to time, that he was having "more fun" at his job than Marge was having at hers.

But he was not the sort of man who came home from a day's work and told his wife to shut up the kids. He was, friends remember, a devoted father—the sort who'd take four little boys for ice cream, the sort who seemed most comfortable with his family.

"He was a diaper changer," says Jan Hoehner, who, with her husband and children, had come to Dayton shortly after the Donahues. "He was an incredibly good family person, and his home life was very important. We'd come over to visit and we'd all sit around the kitchen table and she'd be folding diapers and he'd be folding diapers too, and we'd all have a glass of wine right there, in the midst of the kids."

Still, Donahue was often not home; his schedule was a killer. "Conversation Piece" took him to the station at noon, and he had also become an adept enough announcer to anchor the 6:00 P.M. and 11:00 P.M. WHIO-

TV newscasts. He might come home to grab supper, but two of the kids were in school by now, so he couldn't see them in the mornings, when he wasn't working. And while everybody else was sitting on the porch, he was back at work.

While some wives of broadcasters (for the field was almost entirely male-dominated then) could accept this life, Marge, her friends felt, could not. Adoring as she was, friends said, she felt some resentment at raising four sons and being alone in the evening.

And there was something else. Much as she loved Phil, much as it had been her idea to leave college and marry him (her family would have preferred for her to stay in school), Marge, according to her friends, seemed to be growing discontented.

It wasn't that Phil and Marge lacked material things. The couple had only one car, so that Marge had to drive Phil to work and back in the early years, but they did have a lovely, five-bedroom, split-level home in the suburbs of Centerville, and they could afford to entertain often, which they did. (They both loved card games and noisy parties.)

Still, Marge was becoming restless. Her life was going the way a good Catholic girl's life was supposed to go: she was bearing children—many children—and she was being a helpmate to her husband. She was a good homemaker, a wonderful cook. She entertained, as all her friends agree, beautifully; an invitation to Phil and Marge's was practically a guarantee of a happy evening.

Yet, slowly, Marge began to realize that having baby after baby wasn't enough, and that, while she was a decent enough housekeeper, she had never especially enjoyed cleaning up after everyone in the house. "The Politics of Housework": that was a phrase that would be repeated, from housewife to housewife, across the land then. Women would wonder, picking up their husband's pajamas, their husband's beer glasses, their children's toys, why *they* would always be expected to clean up after doing a full day's work around the house. Or they'd wonder, out at a dinner party, why it was always the women who rose to clear the table, as the men remained seated, smiling beatifically.

Those were the days of the beginning of the woman's movement. Betty Friedan's *The Feminine Mystique,* published in 1963 (the same year Donahue took over "Conversation Piece") had begun to make waves. Women who had before merely accepted the status quo were now starting to ask questions. Why did they address their gynecologists by their titles, while their gynecologists spoke to them using their first names? Why were they always secretaries and file clerks and never the boss? Why were they the nurses, rather than the doctors? Why was it *assumed* they were better with children than their husbands might be?

Phil, always sensitive to trends, was aware of the changes—and the inequities.

He himself had interviewed Friedan on the radio when her book had come out, and he suffered a painful shock of recognition while talking with her and reading what she had to say.

The very first paragraph of her book, in fact, hit home with him.

The problem lay buried, unspoken for many years in the minds of the American woman. It was a strange stirring, a sense of dissatisfaction, a yearning that women suffered in the middle of the twentieth century in the United States. Each suburban wife struggled with it alone. As she made the beds, shopped for groceries, matched slipcover material, ate peanut butter sandwiches with her children, chauffeured Cub Scouts and Brownies, lay beside her husband at night—she was afraid to ask even of herself the silent question—'Is this all?'

Reading it, a terrible thought occurred to Phil: *Friedan could have been describing Marge's day.*

Thinking about the paragraph, he later told the Dayton *Daily News,* a dozen thoughts flashed through his mind. He suddenly realized everyone was "programmed" as male or female by their parents, and that women had been programmed to pursue the sole goal of landing a husband. And that that was not good. "If the sole goal of half the population is to get a man, we're in trouble," he thought. He recalled that when he and Marge were married, the words "love, honor, and obey" were for her only, and that he had really "thought of my wife like an extension of my personality . . . like an adoring Mrs. Ronnie Reagan, forever smiling up at me." He slowly— for this took time—realized that it was Marge who had gotten the scholarships in college, not him; Marge who read more than he; Marge who often came up with the good ideas, while *he* got all the applause.

It was a confusing time for Donahue. He had been raised as a nice Catholic boy, picking up the check, walking the girl home, being more than a little protective.

Now, all of a sudden, he saw that his protectiveness was not only not admired, it was resented. Women saw paternalism and protectiveness as something that put them down; it kept them at home, doing housework, while men were out doing more interesting work. It kept them from being privy to male conversations about politics and economics and other "serious" affairs.

Women now even resented the cozy familiarities that used to be considered flattering.

Donahue saw that quite clearly when he was doing a panel show in Detroit, in 1964. A twenty-year-old woman, in about the fourth row, had a question. He offered her the microphone so she could speak. "Yes, honey?" he asked encouragingly.

"Honey?" the woman said. Donahue still recalls the rage on her face.

"I was very embarrassed, very certain that I'd done something wrong, but not quite sure what," he says. Then it hit him. "Suddenly I realized I didn't know her, that to call her 'honey' was condescending. It was a familiarity that I shouldn't have presumed. I was doing this sexist thing in front of three hundred people. It was a public embarrassment."

It was a painful realization.

Marge, meanwhile, was having some realizations of her own. For one thing, she understood that she had always run her household under a burden of guilt.

"I used to feel that if I left the kids' things laying around the house, it was a reflection on me," Marge would say later. "I have a great aversion to picking up after people. I did it for a long time, because with kids the only alternative is chaos. But I didn't like it."

She made up her mind to change her ways. She announced her plans to Phil. Phil was open intellectually, but emotionally he was having trouble dealing with it all.

That was okay. Marge was an independent woman, with a stubborn streak. When she made up her mind, her mind was made up. She was determined to change the way her family lived—and she got the message across to Phil.

"I knew it was a whole new ballgame when my pajamas were still on the bedroom floor when I came home one night," says Phil.

And it *was* a whole new ballgame. Marge started negotiating for a new way of life, insisting that her husband and children share household chores with her; she wanted a day off from the family, when Phil was to take care of the kids; she instituted family meetings every couple of weeks, in which the tasks were distributed—from bringing up baskets of laundry and sorting them (in the Donahue family, the laundry was twelve to sixteen loads a week!) to taking out the garbage. Phil took on the daily tasks of clearing the table after dinner, loading the dishwasher and vacuuming when a room needed it. Eventually, the two would both join NOW.

But that would be a long time coming. Meanwhile, Phil's talk show would take up a large part of his time. Sacrifices, for Marge and the family, would be involved.

Marge, friends say, had never cared for Phil's late hours, but there was one incident—when she was pregnant with their fifth child—that made her dislike them even more.

It was Phil's birthday, in late December, and Marge, in the couple's only car, had gone to the station with the boys, to pick him up and bring him back for a special birthday dinner. Coming back, with Phil at the wheel, the car in front of them stopped short and Marge slammed into the windshield. The children were shaken but unhurt. Phil was not harmed, but Marge would later require plastic surgery for her injuries.

It's a frightening thing to be in an automobile accident: there you are, in an everyday situation you've come to regard as safe and commonplace, and suddenly you realize how fragile your life is, and the lives of your loved ones. It's a disturbing thing to see someone you love in pain, while you stand helpless and unhurt, nearby.

The sight of Marge, battered and pregnant, would be a hard one for Phil to forget. The accident left him more upset than anyone at the radio station had ever seen him. The man who was usually all business, was this time clearly in distress.

As for Marge, friends said she viewed the accident as yet another unfortunate by-product of Phil's dreadful working hours. If only he'd had a normal work day, she told a woman friend later, this whole thing would never have happened.

Phil, meanwhile, was also beginning to have his own doubts about his job. He may have been a minor celebrity in Cleveland, but in his office he shared a secretary, and certainly did not particularly receive star treatment. WHIO's manager remembered that Phil, in those days, "was always coming into my office, saying, 'I want to be in carpetland, baby.' He meant the executive suite."

He himself was worn out by the late nights, and he was no longer sure the show was paying off, in professional terms. "I felt trapped, I felt I wasn't going any further," he says now, adding that if he hadn't left, "I'd still be doing what I was doing then."

He decided to give it up. But he did not go quietly. On April 15, his farewell to broadcasting appeared as a guest column in the Dayton Daily News. In it, he praised his station: "When I came to Dayton, WHIO had one news car. Now we have four news cars, a helicopter, an airplane, and walkie-talkies . . . but hardware is not the whole story . . . the name of the game is people, and in that we've gone first class." He put forward a few of his beliefs about news reporting, including the theory that, rather than try to get it *first*, to get the 'scoop,' reporters should try to get it *best*—complete and comprehensive.

"How is the community served by the 'just-handed-to-me' report of a child struck by a car . . . no further details available?" he wrote. "Why would it be unprofessional for a reporter to wait the twenty minutes it would take to get a report on the seriousness of the injuries and the identity of the child."

He was, in so many words, favoring the in-depth approach—an approach that would be the basis for his program in years to come.

He also made a case for upping the salaries of newsmen.

"Financially I did fine," he said. "But much of my income came not from being a reporter, but a semi-entertainer. If we really believe that a democracy's strength lies in an informed people, then broadcasting captains must do more for the reporter than brag about him . . . they must pay him . . . disc jockeys make more base pay than reporters. The time is now for the reporter, who has done so much to keep broadcasting's image above water, to share in the industry's golden days of profit."

Then he was off to the business world—that secure, safe place he had planned would be his future in college, then chosen to discard. He joined the E. F. McDonald Company, a Dayton-based corporation that sold sales-motivation programs, in the form of travel or merchandise awards, to other corporations.

Marge, friends report, was "tickled to death" by Phil's job. But for Phil, it was a miserable period. His closest friends recall the time he spent at the company as the low point of his life, one of the few times they would see him depressed for any amount of time. And at McDonald, for the first and only time in his professional life, he would be considered a liability, not an asset.

"He was hired for two reasons," says one of the higher-ups at the company. "He was friendly with the president, and he also claimed that he had a personal relationship with someone who could have been a very big account—Airtemp, the Chrysler air conditioning outfit. We later found out he hardly knew the guy, that this so-called relationship was meaningless; he was assigned to Airtemp about twenty minutes.

"He was a smart enough boy," the man continues, "but it just showed all over him that he was putting in time till something better came along. Nobody took him seriously . . . wasn't a soul that felt he'd be around very long, and he'd also been hired at a salary over what the other guys in the office were making—some of them very experienced salesmen—and that was resented. The women in the office detested him. He was overbearing; for a new guy in the office to be bossing them around, just wasn't smart . . .

"In the nine months he was with us, he never sold anything," the man continued. "That wasn't that unusual. Our business comes in very large hunks; you might make a half-million- or a million-dollar sale . . . also, a fellow coming in is not assigned to the choice accounts, so lack of sales didn't discourage us as much as his very bad work habits. A typical day for Phil's fieldwork was to come in, have some coffee, maybe make a call, then off about that time for lunch with his cronies at the country club, then back to the office to see if there was mail, then about that time it was cocktail hour."

Salvation came for Donahue—though not for his marriage—in the form of an opening at WHIO's competitor, WLWD-TV. They were losing Johnny Gilbert, the host of a local variety show; George Resing, program director at WLWD, remembered Donahue's work from "Conversation Piece." But while Donahue, by all reports, was tremendously unhappy as a salesman, he did not leap at the chance to return to broadcasting.

"I pursued Phil for a long time," says Resing, "but I couldn't get him to say yes. The big problem was Marge, his wife . . . she was into women's lib and resented his career . . . she wanted a private life, and *she* wanted to be a star . . . and he was always very concerned about the marriage. I didn't believe, with the religious background, they'd ever get divorced . . ."

The courtship took months. Resing first met with Phil on a Good Friday, at a Dayton nightclub called Suttmillers, and then, at various times, over dinners with their wives, and in hotel rooms.

"It was really dumb," laughs Resing. "I felt like I was having an affair with him, but he was very concerned about security, very worried that someone at McDonald would find out."

Critical to the wooing of Donahue was the wooing of Marge. "There was great resentment there," says Resing. "She just didn't want it, she felt she was being conned."

To placate Marge as well as her husband, Resing promised that Phil would not have to do the eleven o'clock news. He also gave Donahue his first contract, at $24,000 a year—more money, Donahue says, than he had ever seen in his life.

The deal having been set, the Donahues and the Resings went to the home of WLWD's general manager to celebrate with champagne.

In the outside world, notice was being taken.

The press had always been friendly to Phil, and he, in turn, as a newsman himself, had cooperated with them—and now they praised his return.

The Dayton *Daily News* TV columnist, Gee Mitchell, talking of the new show—and reminding his readers of

Phil's old "Conversation Piece" radio show—said that talk shows were "right down (Phil's) alley and the thing he does better than anyone on the air in these parts, as he has demonstrated on numerous occasions."

CHAPTER SIX:

"The Phil Donahue Show"

Women want more than soaps and games.
　　　　　　—Phil Donahue,
　　　　　　Detroit *News*, February 12, 1978

It's often said of Phil Donahue that he knows the American housewife; that he knows the way a twenty-nine-year-old woman with three children really dresses while some New York designer is off creating absurd outfits for her; that he knows what women really think of extramarital affairs while some fancy East Coast psychologists are lauding "open marriage."

But why shouldn't this be true? For Phil came out of that middle-class Catholic world where women were housewives; he saw—in his own home—an intelligent, creative woman struggling to hang onto her own identity as she shoveled puréed pears into yet another infant's mouth.

He had learne ', from "Conversation Piece," the sort of things women cared about; the sort of subjects that enraged, inflamed, intrigued. When he sat down with George Resing to put "The Phil Donahue Show" together, he had a very definite audience and presentation in mind. Like Phil Donahue, the approach wouldn't be affected, ponderous, or any too refined. But it would be direct.

"The people we want," he said to Resing over and over again, "are the women who slosh diapers."

"The women who slosh diapers"—there's a world of information about housewives in that phrase. It speaks of women who cannot afford Pampers, day in and day out; it speaks of tedium and responsibility; it speaks of the exhaustion of dealing with two-year-olds and their magnificent illogic, and of infants who get up in the middle of the night and scream, while the housewife, with her wonderful education, gets up and takes care of the baby, and her husband rolls over.

It was a world Phil Donahue knew, and a world he intended to reach. He and Resing switched the time slot for "The Phil Donahue Show" (they nicknamed it "The P.D.S.") from nine o'clock to 10:30, to make sure they wouldn't get any children. "And," says Resing simply, "we didn't want any men." They envisioned their viewers as women from eighteen to thirty-four.

They put together a guest list for the show's first six weeks, focusing on the sorts of people Phil had done so well with on "Conversation Piece" (many of the same guests would return to him now). They planned to deal with issues rather than movie stars (this was largely pragmatic; how many movie stars, after all, were going to be coming to Dayton?), and to focus on matters of particular interest to their audience: medical and sexual and romantic matters, certainly, but also controversial new ideas about careers; responsibilities to families; division of labor at home; and religion.

Their guest list for the first week was typical: a local obstetrician who would show films of a baby being delivered; a panel of bachelors, speaking on the single life. (Phil's fellow broadcaster John Lindsey would be on that show, and would later recall that Phil's attitudes toward marriage were "very Catholic—he seemed to feel bachelorhood was an empty life and wonder how one can exist without women and children.") He also lined up a show on the high cost of dying.

Resing and Donahue also began to put together a group of people who would remain with Phil to the present day, among them Dick Mincer, a staff director at the station, and Patty McMillan, then Resing's secretary, who would be trained to handle the incoming phone calls and cue Donahue from a little glass booth.

As for Donahue's set, simple and hexagonal, it would be inspired by a hexagonal ring Resing wore at the time. (Conscious of Resing's part in his success, Donahue even today teasingly calls him "starmaker.")

Then Resing and Donahue had to decide on the guest to kick off the premier show. In broadcasting, that is no small decision. Propelled by curiosity, any number of viewers will give a new show a try. Make your opening show wonderful, and you're off to a wonderful start. Let your show die, and you'll have to struggle like crazy to regain the viewers you've disappointed. As everyone in the business knows, it's harder to change someone's mind than to make a good first impression.

For their premier show, Donahue and Resing decided upon atheist Madalyn Murray, the woman whose lawsuit (Murray vs. Curlett) had resulted in the Supreme Court's ban on prayer in schools.

In these days of gay rights and transsexuals, a staggering divorce rate, widespread drug use, and religious cults from the Moonies to Hare Krishna, atheism seems like tame stuff. But in the early sixties, it was not.

In 1964, in fact, in an article in *Life*, Madalyn Murray referred to herself as "the most hated woman in the U.S." *Life* itself called her "America's most outspoken and militant atheist." A divorcee—which, in those times, did not help her cause—and the mother of two sons, Mrs. Murray's unpopularity was staggering.

A social worker for twenty-one years, she was fired from her job less than a day after she brought her suit against prayer in the schools (her employers charged her with incompetence). And as she continued her work, which included a campaign to tax church properties, her unpopularity grew. Every window in her home had been broken, and her younger son had actually been stoned. Her older son Bill, in whose name she had initiated her suit, had been beaten over a hundred times as the suit went through the courts; her car had been vandalized so often that repair bills ran into the thousands of dollars. Her hate mail was hideous. One letter contained a newspaper photo of Mrs. Murray, smeared with human excrement: "This is my toast for you—here's crud in you eye—and I hope somebody poisons your beer," it read. Another went for the physical. "You must be an insidious creature, without even a brain. No woner you're crazy. You probably have no children either, let alone a man. Your hooked, ugly nose, triple chin, and fat 'slobby body' are enough to make you godless."

Madalyn Murray could dish it out, however, as well as receive it. She was belligerent, fiery, and articulate. "If people want to go to school and be crazy fools, that's their business," she told a reporter. "But I don't want them praying in ball parks, legislature, courts and schools; I don't want to see their religion emblazoned on the public buildings I look at. They can believe in their virgin birth and the rest of their mumbo-jumbo as long as they don't interfere with me, my children, my home, my job, my money, or my intellectual views."

In Dayton, Ohio, a churchgoing community, this was strong stuff. And Murray, in the small WLWD studio on that premier Donahue show, did not back off.

"There have been six attempts on my life in the past four years," she told Donahue. "It's a very exciting existence, living with Christians."

She pointed a finger at the audience. "I think, at one time or another, each of these good people here has doubted the existence of God," she said.

It was a tense moment. This guest was not courting the audience, not going after its approval like a movie star or a new comedienne will on "The Tonight Show," but actually attacking. It was an important moment, an *alive* moment. A lesser talk-show host might have let it pass, or simply savored the moment before moving on to another point. Donahue did not. He used the audience and enlarged on the moment. Would those members of the audience, he asked, who had ever doubted the existence of God, raise their hands.

Not a soul moved. The cameraman panned over the group; still there wasn't a gesture.

Donahue hung in.

"Hasn't any one of you ever doubted?" he persisted.

Pushed, a woman responded.

"Not even for a moment," she said.

Tempers rose. Murray continued her assault. She said churches were "corrupt" and claimed that the federal government daily gave sixteen million dollars to the church.

As on "Conversation Piece," most of the hour was devoted not to conversation between Donahue and Murray, but to callers.

"If you don't believe in God, how can you believe in the powers of nature?"

Not pausing for an instant, Murray replied that that had never been a problem for her. Then she suggested to the caller that a belief in God was a deterrent to pleasure, not something that made the world more beautiful.

"There is a monkey on your back, if you believe in God," she said.

The telephone wires were burning up. The show made the Dayton *Daily News* that day. It was big.

The mail poured in. Whatever Donahue and Resing had concocted for the first six weeks of the show was working.

Dayton, that year, had been ripped apart by a series of race riots; 1967 was a year of unrest in the black ghettos, and of white backlash. Phil Donahue brought on Governor George Wallace, and subjected him to merciless questioning—and encouraged the studio audience to do the same. (The audience was smaller then—eighty people against today's two hundred—but in a way that was better, because it was more intimate.)

Then he brought on prophet Jeane Dixon. No matter that Donahue himself was a cynic—he knew Dixon was an irresistible subject. The housewife, facing a dreary routine of laundry and cooking and getting the kids to school, knowing too well what her own future was, would enjoy hearing someone who proposed to know what lay in store for Jackie Kennedy or the President of the United States. And if, like Donahue, you were a skeptic, it was still fun to hear what this "crackpot" had to say, to yell at the television set and tell Jeane Dixon she was a damn fool, to wait and see if any of her nutty predictions came true. It might be showbiz, it might be entertainment, but as Phil Donahue will admit today, he's never been against a little entertainment now and then.

"We do some showbiz stuff, sure," he says, even

today, "but that's legal. We don't say, 'Ain't it awful!' five days a week. It helps us do the serious stuff on the show the next day."

Yet he had the knack of packaging serious stuff in an entertaining way. He was aware of the tedium of nothing but host and guest sitting on a set debating for an hour ("talking heads," it's called in the industry); so whenever he could, he used visual picker-uppers: short films; exhibitions; a sample, perhaps, of a guest's work. He and his team knew that cutting back and forth to the studio audience made the show more visually interesting—and they also knew that the mounting excitement of a group of people in the studio could feed the viewers' interest. Donahue also knew, like a carnival barker or a politician, how to whip a studio audience into a froth of excitement, how to shock them enough, but not too much—how to make them respond.

And early on—within the first few weeks of the show—he *proved* that he knew, with a show so memorable it made shockwaves as far away as New York.

The subject, innocent enough in itself, was a child's doll. But, oh, what a doll. A little-boy doll, it was being labeled as "anatomically correct," and was going into the stores in preparation for the upcoming Christmas season.

It wasn't crude, it wasn't tasteless. If anything, it was a rather muted, understated facsimile of a baby boy: tiny testicles, a little button of a penis—certainly nothing more than most kids with little brothers had seen one time or another.

Still, if you want to excite the American public, bring up the topic of sex education and kids. Schoolteachers have lost their jobs over that topic. Parents—even normally quiet, polite folks—have become enraged over it. Sex may be all over this culture, in the movies, on the television screen, but let even an innocent representation of nudity, in the form of a little-boy doll, into the toy department, and parents will go wild.

Phil Donahue knew that. He knew, from "Conversation Piece," where the raw nerves lay. And he knew how to deal with the subject for maximum impact. So, early in the show, after the introductory talk was over, he simply held up the doll and showed it to his audience—the eighty women in the studio, the thousands of women at home.

"What do you think of this doll?" he asked.

The studio audience went wild. The viewers at home did also. Phil Donahue still vividly remembers the reaction.

"It was like a bomb had gone off," he said. "The phone company finally got through to say that every phone in downtown Dayton was paralyzed because everyone was calling our show. I just knew then," he said, "we had the formula."

He also had the press. The day after the baby-doll incident, *Variety* ran a front page headline on the show—rather remarkable coverage for a local TV show.

And not three weeks after the show had begun in Dayton, the Dayton *Daily News* was showering Donahue with compliments.

"Phil's doing his part to push the medium up in this area," enthused TV critic Gee Mitchell, adding that in the short time Phil had been on, he'd made "some pretty big waves in the sea of public opinion."

As for Phil, he let it be known that he *thrived* on the controversial, loved it, couldn't get enough of it, chewed it up and ate it for breakfast, and hollered for more.

"Honesty," he told Mitchell, "is the key. We lay it out straight. We're not dodging any issues and don't intend to, as long as they're legitimate. Naturally, we don't agree with everything our guests have to sell. The fact that we're putting them on the air doesn't mean we're buying what they're selling. But we'll let them make their pitch, within reason, then let the viewers have them."

He also discussed the importance of the studio audience, those down-to-earth, pragmatic, horse-sense ladies who, Phil could see even then, were *making* his show.

"Now and then a question is overlooked by the audience, or maybe whoever intended to raise it hasn't been able to get through on the phone lines," he said. "In such cases, I'll bring it up, but this hasn't happened too often yet, which indicates to me that our audience is on its toes. Within the limitations of time and phone lines, they've given each of our subjects a thorough going-over. They've measured up to my expectations all the way, maybe even better than I anticipated they would."

"I owe you." That's a phrase that guests often use to Donahue after the show.

But there's a group of people Donahue himself owes, and whom he knows he owes: those tough, bright, no-nonsense women who make the show sizzle with their startlingly direct questions.

"Without the audience, there's no Phil Donahue," Phil says often, and he has a point.

It was, after all, a member of the home audience, those first years in Dayton, who asked Chet Huntley how old he was; another phone caller asked Tommy Smothers if he believed in God; yet another asked Bob Hope how much Chrysler spent on his show. ("Nobody else would ask a question like that," says Phil.)

It is still a member of the audience who, with a choice

phrase, a succinct down-home delivery, will bring a guest who's talking nonsense back to earth with one deft blow; perhaps a panel of men, on a show on mid-life crisis and male menopause, will refer to extramarital sex as a means of "finding themselves," and then one smart housewife will take the microphone. "Isn't this just a fancy excuse to have an affair?" she asks.

And Donahue—who knows his audience—steps close beside her, takes the mike, and allies himself with her. "That's right," he says. "It's pretty hard to feel sorry for ol' Dad, when ol' Dad is sneaking off to the No-Tell Motel."

He's worked that audience; he's used them to build excitement the way an orchestra leader brings up the brass section; he knew when, he knew where, he knew how much.

He was doing a show on a sixteen-year-old boy convicted to die in the electric chair for murdering his foster father, and had been debating the death sentence for nearly the entire hour. How to cap the show? Donahue used a technique from the Roman Colosseum: let the audience decide whether the boy was to live or die. First the ladies who wanted the death sentence were to applaud, then those who opposed it. The audience was overwhelming in its applause for the death penalty.

But an enthusiastic audience, Donahue knew, could not provide the whole show; he had to keep it going by continuing to snag controversial guests, and by being exciting himself. Sure, big celebrities would have been terrific, but Donahue didn't have the money, the location, or the name to compete with Carson.

"We couldn't get stars, big names," he says. "That was probably good, in a way. We learned to survive without them. But we still begged them to come. For

two years we begged them to come. Norman Rockwell
would walk into the studio and say, 'What the hell am
I doing in *Dayton?*' "

And if he couldn't make his audience sit up and take
notice by producing a Liz Taylor for them, he could
make them take notice by being a little wild and crazy
himself. If keeping those ratings meant a little showbiz
stuff once in a while, he'd do it—he'd climb into a
bathtub for a dreary show on new bathroom designs;
he'd get out on the floor and do exercises with the sexy,
leotard-draped Gunilla Knutson.

He'd do risky, dangerous stunts as well: he battled
with management at the station to build a big ski jump
in the parking lot, had them fill it with artificial snow,
and then put on his skis and skied down. ("Just about
broke his tush," recalls George Resing, dryly.)

For a show on logrolling, he applied pressure until
a large swimming pool outside the station was filled with
logs, then he got into a wet suit and tried to compete
with the logrollers.

Issues were fine, but Donahue and Resing weren't
about to take any chances; in the early days, if they could
throw in some visual razzle-dazzle to make a point, they
did.

Skydiving was becoming popular? Hell, they'd arrange to have some skydivers parachute into their parking
lot—an area Resing recalls as being "about a big as a
postage stamp."

The anniversary of the assassination of President Kennedy was coming up. They borrowed a car of the same
model as the one Kennedy had been killed in, rented the
same type of rifle, put a few dummies in the car—and
reenacted the horrifying incident to test out an assassination theory.

Still, that sort of thing would finally be a very small
part of the show. For Donahue was committed to the

idea that women wanted something of substance, more than soap operas and condescending game-show hosts, so—for the most part—he stuck to issues.

He kept an eye out for guests with something to say about men and women, and when those guests were outrageous and outspoken, articulate and well educated, he would, always sensitive to his audience, bring them back again and again. Such a guest was anthropologist Ashley Montagu—still a Donahue regular—who had succeeded in angering a good deal of the male population with his book *The Natural Superiority of Women.* Bright and argumentative, impressive and authoritative-sounding with his clipped British accent, Montagu was a natural for Donahue.

Arriving in Dayton the evening before a show, Montagu might announce to the press that family size should be regulated; energetic and persuasive on Phil's show the next morning, he would stick to his guns and add that women should be encouraged to go into public life because they were "quicker on the uptake, more compassionate and understanding than men."

This is, in itself, a compelling statement. But Donahue has never been one to let a situation—or a statement—remain static. As an interviewer, he always pushes the subject into even stronger statements by asking the tough question, the leading question.

"I think you would vote for a woman just because she is a woman," Donahue said.

The gray-haired anthropologist admitted he would.

But would there, during their lifetimes, ever be as many women in politics as men? Donahue pursued.

"There will never be the same proportion of women because the larger number will select to be homemakers," said Dr. Montagu, adding his own particular theory that women could achieve greater gratification in the family, because they were thereby involved in the welfare of others. (It would have been interesting, at about this time, to have heard what Marge Donahue had to say about that.)

Theories like *The Natural Superiority of Women* were frightening to many people. But in doing his show, Donahue was not only shaking up others, he was also often bringing himself face-to-face with his own fears, shaking himself up.

The show? Again, nothing shocking by today's standards—just, for instance, a homosexual talking openly about his life. But ten years ago, in the days when a man could lose his job if it was learned that he was gay (something that, in fact, still happens today), it was a shocking show.

"A homosexual on the show . . . was considered revolutionary," Phil told *TV Guide*. "I was so scared. A gay in 1968. We got hundreds of calls. And then it happens; a woman calls in and says to the gay, 'How does Phil look to you, hmmmmmm?' My career passed before my eyes. I felt, oh my gosh, everyone is going to think I'm gay. That's what you were afraid of then."

It was a wild show, a show where the audience soon learned that anything could happen. In the early days of the show, Donahue acquired a taste for going on location, and that made it even more spontaneous and exciting.

In one case, the show even got raided.

It happened when Phil decided he just had to do an interview with a local motorcycle gang called the Outlaws. A mean-looking gang, given to wearing black leather and torn T-shirts and the obligatory Iron Cross, the Outlaws were a rough bunch, frequently in trouble with the law.

Still, Phil was determined he would talk to them on camera, and he also decided that the show would have more impact out of the studio, on their turf. Accordingly, he and his camera crew arrived at one Drexel Cafe, on West Third Street. It was dangerous stuff. At about the same time, a West Coast author, who had lived with a motorcycle gang, had been beaten within an inch of his life.

This group, however, was benign—to Phil. And they were eager for attention. Twenty of them came to the cafe to talk with him, and some even brought along their girlfriends. But the interview was never completed. Half an hour into it, ten Dayton policemen ran in and arrested three members of the gang. The charge was not pretty: gang rape. The cops were tough. And throughout the arrests, the camera kept rolling—and Phil Donahue's viewers got to see it all. A *real* police story. Once again, "The Phil Donahue Show" made *Variety*.

No question now, the show was hot. Seven months after it had gone on the air, Avco Broadcasting began syndicating it, taking it to Cincinnati and Columbus. Other cities picked it up, and as time went by, other stations around the country bought the show. That did not mean, however, that the show moved ahead at a steady, unbroken climb.

It was carried briefly in New York on WPIX, but running at 11:00 P.M. Sundays it went nowhere, and was soon dropped. It was carried for a year in Washington, D.C., on that city's Channel 7, and suffered the ignoble fate of being dropped after having been wiped out of the ratings by "The Flintstones." (In its last weeks at that station, Donahue hit a rating of one, which meant it was being seen by eight percent of the people who were watching television at the time; "The Flintstones" was, on the other hand, bringing in a rating of five, with thirty-eight percent of the television audience tuning in.)

Mostly, though, the show was packing a wallop. And the times did not hurt. It was the sixties, after all, when everything was changing. The women's movement had begun, blacks were taking a militant position, and the Black Panthers were a strong political force. The college kids of the day, as opposed to college kids of Phil's day, were questioning everything, experimenting with drugs, marching on Washington to oppose the Vietnam War. Strange new words crept into our consciousness. There were "hippies" and "Yippies" and "be-ins" and "love-ins." There were "uppers" and "downers" and "speed" and "acid" and "hash." There were kids stuffing flowers into the rifles of National Guardsmen; there were National Guardsmen—in Phil's own state—shooting kids. There were exotic urban outposts on either coast that were becoming counterculture capitals: Haight-Ashbury in San Francisco, the East Village in New York. There were communes and strange eastern religions and exotic, bearded gurus. There were college boys—even nice, midwestern college boys—suddenly sporting shoulder-length hair and ponytails, driving around in Volkswagen vans.

And the situation was no longer "New York and California vs. Everybody Else in the Country"—the changes were all over. One only had to walk through downtown Dayton or Cleveland to see some Good Old Boy yelling to some longhair, "Hey, what *aaaare* yew? A boy or a girl?"

Phil Donahue, the man who had always been on top of the trends, was aware of all that. He knew that it was the children of his midwestern viewers who were running off to Haight-Ashbury or some Colorado commune—or maybe just turning on to drugs at home. And he dealt with it as graphically and dramatically as he knew how.

Phil did a two-part show on drugs and teenagers, and featured as guests Father Daniel Egan, a New York clergyman known as "the junkie priest," who ran a haven for female drug addicts, *and* a seventeen-year-old girl, who had been hooked since she was twelve.

And to get maximum response from the audience, he chose the group that could best relate to the girl's problems: local high school students. The technique worked. As the girl talked of seeing her boyfriend die from an overdose of drugs, the kids looked on in horror—which the television camera caught.

Still, Donahue was not always so successful in capturing the mood of the sixties. In one case, a local black activist, Dr. Arthur Thomas, was invited on the show. Young and aggressive, Dr. Thomas meant business from the moment he arrived. A WLWD staffer, Joyce Andrews, recalls that he took one look at the white female receptionist and threw out a challenge. "Why isn't a black girl sitting there?" he asked.

When he got to Phil, he was still cooking—he talked, all right, but with his back turned to Phil for the entire show. It was a rough one.

And interviewing one counterculture hero of the time—Jerry Rubin—Donahue was absolutely tonguetied. He refers often to that program. On one Johnny Carson show, he called it his "toughest moment in television." On special occasions—like the tenth anniversary of his show, when the crew put together a potpourri of old tapes—the staff always includes the famous Rubin episode, just to tease their boss. It was, after all, live television at its wildest—and, for Donahue, its most embarrassing.

The year was 1969, and Phil was going great guns—and so was Jerry Rubin. A hippie, and then a Yippie, Jerry had marched on the Democratic Convention in Chicago in 1968 with Abbie Hoffman, Tom Hayden, and Rennie Davis, in an attempt to bring the convention to the people and the streets. For those actions, Rubin became a defendant in the highly publicized Chicago Seven trial, in which the defendants were charged with conspiring to incite riots.

It was also Jerry, in those days of American-flag pants and hash pipes, who was the comic relief of the Left. Jerry was the Movement clown, dramatic and colorful and unpredictable. He threw dollar bills from the visitors' gallery of the New York Stock Exchange (the crowd of confirmed capitalists nearly rioted); he appeared before the House Unamerican Activities Committee—that austere group by which Bella Abzug was once ordered to remove her hat—in Vietcong pajamas, painted chest, beret, and even once as Santa Claus. He threatened to put LSD in the Chicago water system (many soft drinks were consumed that week), he tried to levitate the Pentagon, and during the Chicago Seven trial, in which one of the defendants was bound and gagged, Rubin appeared in judicial robes, in an attempt to mock the court.

And Jerry certainly wasn't cleaning up his act for television. In one show that year, in Canada, he ripped off his shirt and stripped to the waist; in another show, the Dorothy Fuldheim show in Cleveland, he announced that the Black Panthers were more moral than the police, and his hostess threw him off the set.

Donahue simply got average treatment, by Rubin's standards—and he was not ready for it.

Yes, Donahue knew Rubin's reputation; yes, he knew that he was the author of a book, *Do It*, which advocated revolution. Rubin was appearing on his show that day to plug that book, in fact.

But prior to airtime, everything seemed normal. Donahue small-talked with Jerry and told him how hard it was to get guests to come to Dayton; Jerry seemed pleasant enough, like any other young author.

Then it was showtime, and everything changed.

Rubin, in his beard and jeans, was suddenly ridiculing Donahue in his three-piece suit, making fun of his hair, comparing him and his politics with Nixon.

Donahue had dealt with unexpected comments for years now—even back on "Conversation Piece," there had been some shockers—but this time he went blank. He could not respond to Jerry's outrageous, rapid-fire comments. He was going blank trying to deal with Rubin's theories. He was falling into a talk-show host's nightmare, the sort where the show has gotten completely away from him. The guest has taken over and is making him look like an ass, and all his intelligent commentary, the stuff the daily press so loves, dries up. And there he is, stammering like a camera-shy amateur, "Uh-huh, uh-huh . . . uh . . ." said Donahue.

Finally, Rubin delivered the coup de grace: "You say 'uh' a lot," he said. "Do you have an anal problem?"

That was it. The home team was routed. The score was Rubin: 9, Donahue: 0. Or, as Donahue himself admits, "The old image of the guy who could handle anything went out the window."

He was shook up, he was angry. Rubin, who's mellowed a bit since those days, remembers that after the show, Donahue wasn't friendly at all; he was rattled, wounded.

But, adds Jerry, there was nothing *personal* in his attack. He had merely thought it the politically correct thing to do.

"I don't remember all of it exactly," he says today. "I mean, Phil Donahue was in Dayton then, and who was Phil Donahue? You know what I mean, I mean I didn't know he was gonna be *Phil Donahue*. I thought I was doing a local Dayton talk show . . . The trial was also going on then, and I was speaking at the University of Dayton, and I figured I'd kill two birds with one stone, sort of . . . And then I went out on the show, and I think he didn't expect to have somebody so powerful. But *I* thought the show was great, I felt it was real television. I thought with the war going on and racial conflict, that what was important was not whether the show was good or not; what was important was emotional truth in television." He continues, in nonstop, high-energy Rubin fashion, "I was tryin' to act real, y'know," he says. "To break the boundaries of television, to say 'this is what I believe in,' and bring some reality into the situation. And what I did on that show was nothing compared to what I did to David Frost. There, I loaded up the studio audience with friends, and then they came out of the audience and squirted everybody with water pistols and took over the whole show. For *that,* we were deported from England."

For what Rubin did, you would think he would be deported from Donahue. But he was not. in 1976, when Rubin published his second book, *Growing (Up) At Thirty-seven,* Donahue invited him to come back on.

Jerry was a different man; he was clean-shaven, short-haired, dressed in a sports jacket. He'd been through just about every new-wave therapy in America: meditation, modern dance, est, Silva Mind Control, Fisher-Hoffman, Swami Raj-ji, Reich, gestalt, bioenergetics, acupuncture, Esalen, Arica, tantric yoga, and t'ai chi—as well as jogging and golf. ("For a man who helped to teach a whole generation to be skeptical of their elected representatives in government, he seems to accept anything that calls itself therapy," a New York literary critic would later say of Jerry.)

Jerry had become less "radical," more "conservative." He was, in the manner of authors, eager to tell all. Donahue said he was eager to listen.

But first, Donahue said, he had a little surprise. "I

want to show you something," he told Jerry.

Then he rolled the film—twenty minutes of the old Jerry Rubin.

"I'd forgotten," admits Jerry, "how heavy it was."

Jerry says he wasn't embarrassed by the tape—though the tables had certainly been turned. During the show, he and Phil talked, together this time. Afterward, they went to lunch.

Donahue talked about how shaken up he had been that first time in Dayton, how he'd lost control and been terribly bothered about it, how angry he'd been at Jerry, but now no longer was.

Jerry told him that he felt the show had been appropriate then. "The country had been at war," he says of those times now. "In 1969, it was healing. I decided to go around to all the people I'd warred with."

The two came back to the office. There was a picture on Donahue's wall that brought back memories. It was a picture, says Rubin, that *was* that show: Jerry, bearded, excited, with his hands raised, Phil sitting there bewildered. Rubin admired the picture. Phil took it off the wall—frame and all—and gave it to him.

"Take it," he said. "I have another one."

Today there is no bad blood between them. Quite the opposite.

"I love his show," says Rubin. "It's so intelligent, it's so real, you get to the issues . . . to go on the show for an hour and deal with one subject is so above the mediocrity and triviality of television. You turn on that show and you learn something. The rest is all crap. If it weren't for a 'Phil Donahue Show' and a Walter Cronkite news, I would throw away my television."

CHAPTER SEVEN:

The Backstage Phil, at the Office/at Home

He's a wonderful man... just his attitudes were better than any other man. For instance, we had this list of whose turn it was to make coffee. It wasn't just me on it, everybody took a turn, including Phil. And that was Phil's idea.

—Mrs. Hazel Dyer, Phil's secretary, on Phil

People came up to my wife and said, "Isn't he wonderful? Do you know how lucky you are?" But I wasn't always so wonderful. There were lots of times she thought she was very unlucky. I bring as much excess baggage to a relationship as anybody.

—Phil Donahue on Phil, *Esquire*, January 30, 1979

Every person who works in front of the public has a mask, an image, and if they are clever, and if they are successful, they work to maintain it. Bing Crosby, in his later years, refused to be photographed without his wig; Jacqueline Onassis, in the years when she was Jacqueline Kennedy, used to make her incoming airplane circle the airport while she fixed her makeup—and though she smoked heavily, she was never photographed smoking a cigarette. Henry Winkler, the television star who, as "the Fonz," is the heartthrob of thousands of teenage girls, was the same about cigarettes.

"I'll give you anything you want, fellas," he said to a group of photographers at a press conference once, as he puffed away, "only please don't take any pictures of me smoking. I've got a lot of kids out there looking up to me."

That's the cosmetic part of a public image; often it goes deeper and becomes more complicated than that. Though the image is supposed to come out of the person, the image starts *determining* the person. The actor who plays Superman really starts feeling that he should protect people because he *is* a little stronger; or a cowboy star, after years of acting in good-guy roles, really begins believing he's the good guy (never mind those years of cheating on his wife); he punches out men who make fun of cowboys, he never swears, he *becomes* his image.

Phil Donahue, in the Dayton years when his show was becoming more and more successful, had a public image also. He was beginning to be thought of as a liberal, open-minded man who was sympathetic to the growing demands of blacks and women. He was viewed as a practicing Catholic who wanted reforms and change in the Catholic Church, a parent who wanted integration in the schools and equal education for blacks and whites. He was a mover in the community, not just on television—someone whose opinions were sought. When Pope Paul VI, in 1968, banned birth control for Catholics, Phil Donahue was among the prominent Catholics who were asked about the issue. "Now that the Pope has polarized the problem, I think the priests will stand up publicly and say they cannot in conscience agree with him. Some will find it impossible to be a Catholic and oppose the Pope. Others will struggle along in opposition," said Phil—cleverly not expressing his own view on the subject. And the interviewer—less clever—did not push him. He was also regarded as a casual fellow, a down-home guy, an informal—no, let's put it bluntly— a *lousy* dresser.

But was the man who was regarded as a feminist *really* a feminist around the home and the office? Was the public humanist always that decent to the people he worked with? When it came to open housing, did this man who admitted he'd grown up in an all-white world really want a black man next door?

Reports vary.

The image of Phil as a fellow who didn't care much about how he looked, and cared even less about fashion, was based in fact, everyone agreed.

George Resing was forever reminding Phil to get a haircut ("He only thought about the show," says George, "he didn't think about anything else."), and his staffers were often appalled at the way he dressed.

In fact, Phil didn't really start looking sharp on television until he had Oleg Cassini as a guest, who took one look and decided something had to go.

"He was wearing, I think, some kind of plaid jacket with flannel pants and a tie I didn't particularly like," said Cassini, in his New York offices, of that early show. "I talked to him after the show, and I tried to be . . . mmmm . . . diplomatic . . . I cannot remember verbatim every word I said, but I know I told him I could make him the Jackie Kennedy of the talk shows. I said, 'You're a good-looking man, you've got a good body, a good face, you've got the raw material, why don't you do something with it?' . . . his response was, 'Fine, we're

Phil Donahue
A MAN FOR ALL WOMEN

PHILLIP J. DONAHUE
B.B.A. in Commerce
Canton, Ohio
University Theatre
Student Senate Public
Information Committee
Y.C.S.

THOMA
B.S. i
Lynchbu
Knigl
Danc
(Fi
Hall

Phil's Notre Dame yearbook identifies him as a
business major. But by graduation day, he had decided
his future was in broadcasting.

Phil in his early broadcasting days in Ohio.

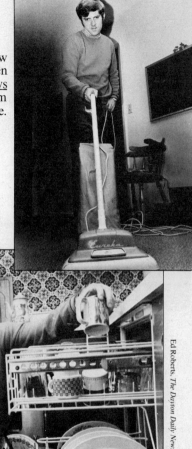

Phil showed how
liberated he was, when
<u>The Dayton Daily News</u>
did a feature on him
and Marge.

"He rubs shoulders with the famed, but does chores at
home," said <u>The Dayton Daily News</u>, when their local
celebrity posed for this shot.

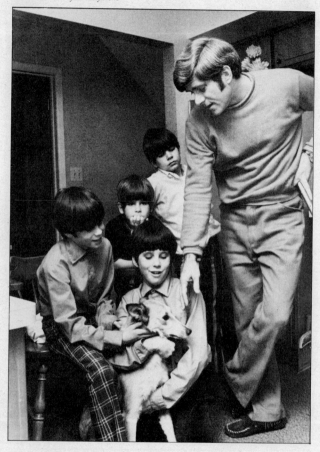

Donahue and sons when the family lived in Dayton.
Casual Phil wears moccasins.

At parties, friends noticed, Phil always gazed
lovingly at his wife Marge. "He always deferred to her,"
said one woman.

Phil's ex-wife Marge and his only daughter, Mary Rose.

Walt Kleine, *The Dayton Journal-Herald*

Donahue, an active sportsman, hits a ball at the
Robert F. Kennedy Pro-Celebrity Tennis Tournament,
held in New York. Once an unknown TV reporter, he's
now considered as big a draw as the movie stars.

Phil and Marlo.

partners, buddy.' One of his greatest human charms is that he is really capable of using the expertise of other people and being humble . . . he admits his own limitations, which makes him, in total, a very big person . . ."

Cassini spared no effort. He not only designed Phil a wardrobe, he also labeled the shirts and ties, and gave Phil a chart explaining which went with which.

"There was a sincere attempt to make him 'with it,'" says Cassini. "Now he cuts a very sophisticated figure, but then . . . he was Mr. Everybody. Now, he's Mr. Somebody. Actually, I did the same thing for Johnny Carson one time, too."

As for the more serious parts of his image—the liberal, the humanist, the feminist—there is controversy.

George Resing, who admires Phil enormously, and even today speaks of him as "a giant," admits that certain problems involved in getting along with people, which Phil reportedly encountered doing "Conversation Piece," he brought along to "The Phil Donahue Show" as well.

"He didn't make any friends at WLWD," says George. "He was very single-minded, he wanted to do things his way . . . he had some encounters."

An old WHIO associate, Lou Emm, was cynical.

"He got very involved in causes, but I felt every cause he espoused in human relationships was a vehicle to further his career in broadcasting."

He repeats a story that went around about Phil during the days of black unrest and open-housing struggles in Dayton.

"The man down the block from Phil had his house for sale, and Phil wanted to know if he would sell his house to blacks—Phil had never even said hello to this man before—and the man just slammed the door in his face."

But other reports indicate that Phil—whatever the depth of his sincerity—was trying to live according to the liberal views he espoused.

When the mayor of Centerville, the Dayton suburb in which Marge and Phil lived, held hearings on open housing, the first person in the audience to stand up and urge the passage of the legislation was Phil Donahue. When busing came to Dayton, Phil and Marge had their children participate and, for a brief time, they took into their home a foster child from a minority family. When Phil and Marge's local church, Incarnation Conception, planned to build a larger wing, Phil and Marge led the group within the parish that opposed it, feeling that the money could better be spent building a church for the poor, in their neighborhood. They were both proud that their oldest son Michael—twelve at the time—was pursuing a non-sexist course of study at the local school, Tower Heights. The course was called "unified arts," and included sewing, cooking, woodworking, singing, and painting.

Not that Donahue wouldn't slip once in a while. A few years after his show had begun, he was talking companionably with Dayton *Daily News* reporter Tom Hopkins about his show. Having made the usual pitch about how his show filled the housewife's need for "a certain kind of progressive concept," he went on to explain what made his show different.

"We're fighting a lot of built-in prejudice," he said. "No broads, no band . . ."

Maybe he meant the word "broads" satirically; perhaps it was a throwback to the time, a few years earlier, when he had inadvertently offended a feminist during a show by calling her "honey." Maybe it *was* a male chauvinist slip.

But as far as most of the women he knew at the station felt, he was trying.

Betty Friedan, a frequent guest on his show, says she always felt Phil was "very receptive and tuned in to the women's movement"; that, even in the beginning, he was one of the few men who didn't make fun of her, and who took the issue seriously.

And a lot of the women who work on the show—almost all of whom started in 1967, in secretarial, receptionist, or clerk positions, at a station that wouldn't allow them to wear pantsuits—found that Phil's attitude, among the men they worked with, was rather good. True, he had begun as a chauvinist—but he was learning. And women were moving up on his show. Patty McMillan, who'd come in as George Resing's secretary, had become an associate producer on the show, and one of a handful of women in the country with executive responsibilities in television; and Darlene Hayes, who had come in as Phil's secretary, was also doing more production work.

In fact, McMillan credits the feminist movement—specifically Gloria Steinem—for helping her get up her nerve to tell her bosses that she felt she was capable of handling the job.

"In the beginning, the show was very small, and it was pretty much Phil doing the hosting, Dick (Mincer) producing and directing, and me as a secretary," McMillan said in an interview with the *Chicago Tribune*. "But during the couple of years I was busy typing up orders, I was also paying close attention to what they were doing—watching Phil do his audience warm-up, listening to Dick arrange programs—and every once in a while I would come in with an idea for a show that would eventually end up on the air. And I started thinking,

'Hey, I could do that too.'

"About that time, Gloria Steinem started coming on the show, and the whole feminist movement was building. Much of what I was hearing started me thinking that I wanted to do something more with my life.

"While this was happening, Phil and Dick were looking for a producer. They had hired a couple of guys, but for one reason or another they didn't work out. So every afternoon I would hear their discussion about possible candidates, but they talked in terms of men only. No woman's name ever came up. Here Phil was, doing all these shows on feminism, but he was still a long way from implementing it in his own life.

"While all this was running through my mind, Gloria appeared on the show one morning, and as I was listening to Phil question her, she said this very simple thing that I'm sure she had no idea would affect anyone dramatically. She said, 'If there's something you want, you have to learn to ask for it. Women have to start speaking up.' That was it; that was all she said. But it struck me as something very important.

"So I took Phil and Dick to lunch, and I said to them very bluntly, 'Look, I've sat in the office for all these years and I'd have to be a terrible dummy not to have absorbed what's going on around me, how the show runs, how everything works. More than that, I feel I have some ideas, something I could add to the show, and I think I could do the job you're trying to fill.'

"The response of the two—including the alleged feminist—was, at first, shock. Once they stopped staring at me, Phil looked at Dick and said, 'Gee, I never thought of that.' And Dick said, 'Gee, I never thought of that, either.' Right there, they both agreed to give it a try."

A year or two after McMillan became an associate producer, Darlene Hayes—a divorced woman with two children, a high school education, and a year of business school—was promoted from secretary/clerk to associate producer, also.

The temperamental, moody Phil? Many of the people who worked with him agree that it was there. George Resing says, quite openly, that after a bad show, Phil would be depressed.

"So down, it would tear him up . . . the typical, terribly creative, caring person who hates any kind of less-than-perfect job."

Resing's one-time secretary, Joyce Andrews, concurs.

"When Phil was upset? He was upset every day," she laughs. Charlene Slack, a woman who worked as a publicist on the show, admitted that Phil would come in "yelling and screaming" if the show hadn't gotten enough press, or a listing hadn't made the papers. But, she adds, his blow-ups weren't very frequent, and "he always came back and said he was sorry, or if he wasn't wrong, come back and say *something* . . . and he was usually right."

He was also, Slack insists, a sensitive, caring man. He threw volleyball parties for his staff, for work well done (Marge served as hostess). He was "always very thoughtful of other people in terms of what they had done for the show."

While he may have had a temper, he was loyal to his staff—even at the expense of good press. And he did *not* favor the needs of working men over working women.

Tom Hopkins, the TV reporter of the Dayton *Daily News,* tells of a time when Donahue had to choose between pleasing Hopkins or pleasing Darlene Hayes— who, at the time, was Phil's secretary.

"Redd Foxx was scheduled to be the guest, and the PR girl invited me out to interview him prior to airtime," says Hopkins. "However, Foxx's road manager phoned

Donahue the night before from Cincinnati, where Foxx was appearing at the Beverly Hills Supperclub. Foxx's manager said Redd was wiped out, and would be unable to make the Donahue show, which was scheduled to air at 10:30 the next morning. But Phil insisted that Foxx be there . . .

"When I walked into Donahue's office around 9:30 the next morning, they were still pouring black coffee into Foxx. He was really in no shape to do the show, but they managed to pull it off. There was just enough time for a ten-minute chat with Foxx, and Phil had already promised Darlene Hayes that she could tape a segment with Foxx for her own show." (Darlene also hosted a program on the station, aimed at blacks.)

"The upshot of it is that Phil told Darlene to go ahead, and told me, in effect, 'tough luck.' After being invited to go to the station, I was pretty irked and I stomped out. Later that day, Phil called to apologize. And his logic made sense.

"'I had promised Darlene that she could do her bit, and I felt I had an obligation to her.' And he added, with just as much sense, 'Tom, we've been friends too long to let a thing like this spoil it.' I had to agree, and we remained friends."

But it wasn't just working women to whom Phil seemed receptive; he also went out of his way to help a woman who'd been out of the labor force to become acclimated to the nine-to-five world.

The woman was Mrs. Hazel Dyer. Older than most of the Donahue staff, Mrs. Dyer had been facing that unsettling time that many Donahue viewers face: the time when the children are grown, the husband is working, and the housewife's role seems suddenly less important than it once was.

It's a difficult time for many middle-aged women.

There are no longer children who need to be cared for, no longer as many errands to run. The house needs less cleaning when the children are grown; meals are smaller and easier to prepare; there aren't all those meetings—the PTA, the Boy Scouts, the Saturday piano lessons and Little League games, the *chauffeuring*.

As for the outside world, it may seem menacing. The language has changed, the codes have changed. Men are dating women twenty years their junior; women are sleeping with men they've only just met. There are office machines that simply did not exist twenty-five years ago: fancy photocopy devices, digital adding machines, microfilm files.

There are people to deal with who seem to be from another world. At home, there may have been strangers at the meeting of the school board, but at least there were children in common; at least you could talk about, for instance, problems of drugs in schools, and how the neighborhood has changed. In a work situation, there are young people who've never changed a diaper; what will you talk about with them?

Such was the situation, in part, that Hazel Dyer was facing. Her youngest child was off at college, her husband was doing well; she really didn't need to work. Time was heavy on her hands, but she was resistant to finding a job—a bit timid about it, perhaps. Friends encouraged her. One friend, in particular, owned a local Manpower office and wanted her to try a job, but she refused.

Then, one day, the Manpower friend tried her again.

"I've got something wonderful, something you just can't say no to," the friend said. "A week as a secretary at the Donahue show."

Hazel was uncertain. "I've never even touched an electric typewriter," she said.

But her friend was encouraging, her husband supportive. He brought Hazel an electric typewriter from the office. "I touched the return button, my dear, and I couldn't *believe* what was happening," she laughs. Hazel practiced. She went in the next day. Both Phil and Dick Mincer, who was, by then, executive producer, put her completely at ease, she says.

"They were extremely lenient," she says. "My typing and shorthand were both just awful, but they didn't mind. I went in for a week and they just kept asking me back. It was extremely flattering."

Hazel also remembers Phil as "more like a friend than a boss."

"I was the oldest person in the office, maybe sort of a mother figure, but Phil made me feel just as important as anybody else," she says. "He was devoted, he was kind, he was extremely loyal."

He also never made her feel like "just" a secretary. Going on location is an exciting time on any talk show, and Phil, in the Dayton years, was taking his show on location a lot—his was, in fact, one of the first shows to film inside a penitentiary. Going on location is a tremendous expense for a television show; what with hotel rooms, meals, traveling expenses, usually only key people are allowed to travel. Some talk-show hosts might not consider their secretaries "key people." Some would prefer to keep them back at the office, taking care of the phones and answering letters. But Phil, Hazel says, insisted that she come along when the show went on location—she was part of the team, after all; he needed her and wanted her there. She was *important*.

She also had the opportunity to grow in her job, as had Darlene Hayes and Patty McMillan in theirs. First simply booking the audience, Mrs. Dyer soon found herself warming them up before the show. Suddenly, the woman who'd been worried about her typing skills was talking with a group of women about the subject to be discussed that day, whether it was dangerous American cars (Ralph Nader), or conservatism in American politics (William F. Buckley). Suddenly, she who had been so nervous was helping other women get rid of their nervousness. She whose world had been limited to kids and husband, was chatting with Gloria Steinem and Bob Hope and Cliff Robertson, getting Phyllis Diller a cup of coffee, making sure Sharon Rockefeller was at ease. ("I *am* kind of a ham," she laughs.) Eventually she even went on the air, doing a cooking show—"Home on Saturday." (It was a non-sexist cooking show, designed for the working woman *and* man!)

When the show later moved on to Chicago, Mrs. Dyer chose to stay with the station, not move on with the show. (Her husband was working in Dayton, and that was her home, after all.) But she remained in contact with Phil, and when she retired three years ago, "The Phil Donahue Show" flew her and her husband Bill out to Chicago, put them up at the Hyatt, and Phil personally showed them around.

"We went to the Ninety-Fifth Club, we went to the Ritz for cocktails, we had dinner at Phil's house one night—that was before he and Marlo were going together—and he cooked. He'd been working all that morning on a dish out of Julia Child, chopping and cooking and sautéing. It was a marvelous weekend," says Mrs. Dyer.

She just can't praise him enough, his former secretary adds; he's a good person, a good friend, a marvelous father. But beyond that, he gave her something very important: the support to build for herself a more fulfilling life.

"I had not worked for twenty years when I went to

that office," says Mrs. Dyer. "I'd stayed at home all the time my family was growing up. I had been living only for my own family. And then I became a person in my own right. I turned my life completely around. And I'd like to just tell other older women—if they give up, it's ridiculous."

All well and good.

But when it came to Phil's ability to deal with a woman in his own home who wanted a life of her own, there were problems. For while Phil was trying to be a liberated man, and acknowledge his wife's needs for a life of her own, he was still aware that he had conflicts.

And his audience knew.

"I remember him once saying on the air that even though he knew it was wrong, he still wanted all women to be barefoot and pregnant," recalls Resing's wife Jane. "I thought it was so honest of him to admit it. He was really fighting it [the old values], and he felt most men felt the same way."

Phil was well-versed in the women's movement. He had had on the show Kate Millett, author of *Sexual Politics;* militant feminist Robin Morgan; and NOW president Wilma Scott Heide. At home, he was doing housework, clearing the table, loading the dishes. When the interviewer for the "Home & Family" section of the Dayton *Daily News* came to interview Marge and Phil ("He Rubs Elbows of Famed, But Does Chores at Home," the headline said), Phil said all the right things about the plight of women: ". . . how really on the ropes a divorced woman is . . . she has the kids, the wage scale becomes critical . . . and there is the divorced male with freedom of choice to go anywhere."

He went on and on, sounding more sympathetic to the single girl than even Helen Gurley Brown.

"There are so few responsible guys around in their thirties or forties," he said, "and how does a woman meet them?"

He could admit his errors publicly—that, for example, while he had gotten guest Johnny Bench's autograph for his four boys, he had not thought to get an autograph for his daughter, Mary Rose, as well. "Now she's mad at me," he said, "and I don't blame her."

He could admit that he often thought his success would be enough for Marge, and he did not mind Marge's teasing. "My success is your happiness," she chanted.

But even with their new jargon, and even with Phil loading the dishwasher, and Marge's day off, there were still inequities. Marge, a creative and intelligent woman, played guitar and worked with ceramics (she was evidently trying out a new name during that time, and signed her work "Margo"), and had informal consciousness-raising sessions with other women. But it was finally she who ran the kids around town, she who cooked the meals, day in and day out.

And even without her restlessness and the feminist issue, there were, friends felt, other problems.

One was Phil's success.

Success, in the abstract, sounds fine. But the reality of being married to a famous person is something else again. It means that what were once intimate moments are no longer private. It means that all sorts of strangers presume intimacy. It means that everyone wants a piece of the celebrity's hide. There are constant invitations to benefits, to charity functions, to community events.

Marge had always savored her privacy. She had opposed Phil's return to broadcasting because she feared it would infringe on that privacy and take him away from home. And she was right—their privacy had been invaded. Quiet family moments were no longer.

Phil's hours were also no pleasure for Marge. He was not even doing the six o'clock news anymore, and his schedule was close to a nine-to-five, but he admits that he was a workaholic. He was absorbed in his job ("tunnel vision" he calls it), and he *did* bring his work home. Marge resented that, and might occasionally make a cutting remark to her family about how Phil would come home from a hard day's work, go into the bedroom, shut the door, dial Bobby Kennedy, and spend an hour on the phone with him, trying to get him to come to Cleveland.

But was the workaholism the basis of the breakup? Donahue, in frequent interviews, suggests it was; Marge refuses to discuss it.

Five years into the Donahue show, the couple were having fights serious enough for Marge to pack and go off to Albuquerque. Five years into the Donahue show, Phil Donahue, the public man, was a tremendous success, syndicated all over the country, but at home, he was troubled and unhappy.

CHAPTER EIGHT:

Breaking Up, Moving On, Dating

> When I grew up, people who got divorced were
> failures. They were almost "fallen." But my big-
> gest fear was losing the children, not seeing them
> grow up.
>
> —Phil Donahue,
> *Chicago Tribune Magazine*,
> May 14, 1978

The winter of 1973-74 was an emotionally trying time
for Donahue. But then, 1973 had been an exhausting
year, a year of much uncertainty, a year of tension.

At home, the disagreements between Phil and Marge
were becoming more and more frequent. And at work,
there seemed to be a different plan every moment; in
April he was riding high, the show having been syndicated in fifty cities. By July, Donahue had taped a series
pilot for CBS—he took his vacation to do it—with the
possibility of doing the show in California. It was a
possibility he apparently felt ambivalent about. It wouldn't
just mean disrupting his family's lives; it would also
mean a change in the show that he wasn't sure he wanted.
His old format, simple and spare, was the one he was
comfortable with. The new one would include an or-

chestra and several guests. And there would be no phone calls. Phil had always done well with the average American housewife. He often admitted to feeling uncomfortable with show business people. He just wasn't certain the new show would be right for him. But on the other hand, it was possibly—the way "Conversation Piece" had been—a time to make a move in his career. Perhaps he had gone as far as he could go with "The Phil Donahue Show" in Dayton, perhaps the format was becoming tired, perhaps it was only a matter of time before people grew weary of him and his down-home manner. But maybe they had the right combination, and should stick to it. Phil truly was concerned about preserving the feeling of community that an audience provided.

"We have to worry about going Hollywood," he said. "We don't want to have that happen to us. We want to enjoy the benefits of originating in a major production area like Los Angeles, but we have to keep our Dayton philosophy."

There was no question that moving to California would benefit the show. There would be more celebrity guests, easier access by everyone. But Marge had already uprooted her life for Donahue, and she wasn't, friends said, crazy about uprooting again and again. And Phil was torn—committed to his marriage, committed to his career—he didn't know what to do.

Meanwhile, plans kept changing. By October, with the show's syndication dropped from fifty cities to thirty-eight, there was talk of moving the show to New York, on the ABC network. There was also talk that Phil would then host the local seven-to-nine news show (a situation that would have been reminiscent of his killer schedule back during his radio days, when he did both the talk show and two late-night news shows).

ABC in New York wasn't the only possibility, though. WNEW, the Metromedia-owned station in New York, was interested in Phil, and WCKT, the NBC affiliate in Miami, was also interested. (Phil and his staff had twice done shows out of WCKT.)

New York, Miami—again, it would mean uprooting the family. And for what? Miami was at least a city where the kids could have a backyard. In New York, the public schools would be awful; they might end up paying three thousand dollars a year, per kid, for private school. Would an Albuquerque-bred woman like Marge enjoy New York? Would it be safe for the family? Army wives are used to moving; some broadcasters' wives get used to it and accept it; but Marge had never been that crazy about being a broadcaster's wife.

Still, with the show losing viewers and syndication down, Donahue was not in his position of greatest power—he had to make an intelligent career choice now.

A career man or woman's identity is very tied up with what they do. Their egos oftentimes rise and fall with the success of a project. Donahue was going through a time of uncertainty with his job in 1973.

And by early fall of '73, he was going through perhaps the most trying time of his life, for he and his wife were separated—he remaining in Dayton, she and the kids back with her family in Albuquerque. She had decided their move was not going to work.

The separation was no secret. People at the station knew, people in the street knew. There were letters to the editor in the newspaper: "I was down to Cincinnati about three weeks ago," a married woman wrote in, "and I saw a piece in the paper that Phil Donahue's wife has left him. Is this true? I hope not." And the paper, the Dayton *Daily News*, made a reply: "A spokesman for Avco Broadcasting in Cincinnati says Phil and his wife,

Margie, are 'trying the separation bit.' Mrs. Donahue is now living in Albuquerque, N.M., the spokesman said, 'but there are no plans for a divorce.' The Donahues have five children."

Separation is painful for anyone. It's particularly difficult when you're a public figure and everyone knows your marriage has just broken up. You have to go to work and, even though you're upset, look happy, put on a good show. You're known to strangers who are not known to you, strangers who may be thinking, "Hey, his wife just left him—wonder how he feels?"

And Phil, all his friends agreed, was not designed for a single life. He had lived alone for maybe six months in his life, between college and marriage. He enjoyed domesticity. He had openly adored Marge; many of their friends not only thought them a loving couple, but spoke of the adoring looks Phil cast in Marge's direction at parties.

"Phil deferred to her all the time," says Jane Resing. "He liked her."

Phil's secretary at the time of the separation, Hazel Dyer, sums up the time of the separation simply, though she and Phil talked about it for hours and hours.

"He was devastated," she says.

Why not? A person lives with another person for sixteen years, through the out-of-work years and the glory years; a person has children with another person; shares a common belief with them in the ways of the universe; gets used to the sounds of the family: the sounds of sons squabbling, of running water in the bathroom, of the kids brushing their teeth or getting a late-night snack. There is the terribly comforting knowledge that when you come home from work, no matter what the hour, there will be people in your home, and a person in your bed. And even if that person in the bed is asleep when you get there, it's a person who knows you, who knows your history. It's a person who protects you from the awful isolation of moving through the days alone; someone to share your ups and downs, someone who's there to help you.

Phil had always had close relationships with people, from the time he was a little boy. He could come home and discuss his feelings with his mother when he was growing up, with his college roommate at school, with Marge all of his adult life. Now she had gone home to Albuquerque. And a nice Catholic boy—who had come, like his wife, from a world where people simply did not get divorced—was looking divorce square in the eye. And it was hard.

Still, there is one good thing about success. If you cannot bear to be alone, it generally gives you a wider range of options. There are all sorts of people who want the company of a single successful man for dinner, all sorts of people eager for the chance to amuse you.

Phil still had his work, and it would help carry him through this period. And he still had all those dinners and benefits to attend, if he wanted. And, faced with that big, empty-feeling house to come home to, he accepted more and more.

One night in early December, he went to the Dayton Advertising Club's roast—one of those peculiar American rites where the idea is to invite someone you especially care for, and then insult them. (Perhaps it's easier for some people to express affection with insults, but if so, it's a curious phenomenon, and one that might bear investigation on the Donahue show.)

The group, that night at the very beginning of the Christmas season, was raucous and enthusiastic. News director Ed Hart was there, WHIO General Manager Stan Mouse, honchos from the Advertising Club, and lots of Donahue co-workers.

One local wit called Phil, that night, "The Soupy Sales of the hysterectomy set" (feminist consciousness had a long way to go at the Advertising Club), WLWD exec Ray Colie teased him on his classy new showbiz style. "A guy who walks crooked and uses three hot combs to fluff his hair up," said Colie. Still another television exec said he could not comprehend the success of a guy like Phil, who, he claimed, went in for subjects like "Ninety-nine Ways to Make Love to Your Husband—Or A Good Friend."

No one had the bad taste to make any "wife" jokes.

Still, it was a grim Christmas for Phil.

And the year to follow would be even rougher, for in February of 1974, just a few weeks after what would have been their sixteenth anniversary, Marge sued Phil for divorce.

The grounds? "Extreme cruelty and gross neglect of duty."

"Plaintiff says that she has been a good and faithful wife," the divorce papers read, "but that the plaintiff has been guilty of gross neglect of duty and extreme cruelty in the manner and in the particular which will be made known to the Court in the final hearing of this action."

The papers spoke of the couple's five children, then aged fifteen, fourteen, twelve, ten, and nine; of their joint property—the 1970 station wagon, the 1972 Mercedes (interestingly enough, for an alleged feminist, both cars were registered in Phil's name), their bonds, their home at 209 Pleasant Hill Court, in Centerville.

Then, in the succinct way of divorce papers, they got to the point:

"Plaintiff prays for a divorce," they read, "that she

be awarded temporary and permanent alimony; that she be awarded exclusive custody, care and control of said minor children of the parties; that she be awarded child support for the five minor children of the parties; that she be awarded equitable distribution of the property of the parties; and for such other and further relief to which she may be entitled, including reasonable attorney fees and costs of this suit."

She also demanded that Phil vacate their home.

Within two weeks, Phil's attorney challenged the suit, in a cross-complaint for divorce. On behalf of his client, he denied that Donahue had been guilty of gross neglect or extreme cruelty, and alleged that Marge, however, had been cruel and neglectful, and demanded a divorce—and custody of the children.

It was going to be a battle, no question. And not a month after it was begun, Phil's life was further complicated. He and the show's staff would be moving, as of May 1, to Chicago.

Psychologists and sociologists, who often make a business out of calculating the unmeasurable, have done a great deal of research into human stress. According to that research, death of a mate, divorce, and loss of a job—through firing—are among the most traumatic and stressful occasions for an adult. Change of job and moving to another city are also high on the list. Interestingly, reconciliation is viewed as nearly as stressful as separation. A period of reconciliation is, after all, a tense time. There is fear that the union will break up again; old angers to deal with; the terrible anxiety of not knowing. With a separation—in which both parties definitely want out—though the pain may be higher than that of a reconciliation, the tension is often lower.

Phil's life, that May, was reportedly tense. Though he was not changing his job, he was changing his professional environment, moving into a more sophisticated, more competitive town. True, he had moved around a lot the year after graduating college, but that was very different; he had little to lose, moving about was expected and he had someone who loved him. He also had his faith when he was young, a belief in the Catholic order of things. Now, he had long been doubting many of the givens of the Catholic Church—including the infallibility of the Pope and the ban on birth control—and he had begun to think that his living by Catholic rules had been a wasted effort. The Church was not the support it had once been. As for his marriage, it seemed to be on again, off again; not until, friends say, Phil moved to Chicago alone, was he seen doing his show without his wedding ring.

Then, suddenly, there was news; the ring was back on. In June, the divorce suits, at the request of both parties, were dropped. As of late summer of 1974, Marge and Phil were living in an enormous house in the posh Chicago suburb of Kenilworth, a house that someone close to Marge—though he admits he never saw it—describes as a "blighted sepulchre."

"One of those places like the Chivas Regal commercial," says that report. "Drapes falling off the windows, one of those overbuilt homes of the thirties. Donahue paid a bundle for it. And into that house they moved, in an attempt to rescue the marriage. I don't know how much of a joint effort it was buying it, I know Marge was never really happy there . . ."

The purchase of a large house, when a marriage is going badly, is not unusual. Neither is the decision to have a baby, to take a trip, to try life in another city. The logic is: we will try this new thing; it will bring us together; it will somehow make our life different; it will fix the shambles our life has become. Or: we will buy this beautiful house, which will be our dream house, and living in this beautiful house, everything will be magically all right. Or: *I* will buy this beautiful house, my wife will see how hard I have worked, my wife will see how much I love her, and everything will be all right.

But fix-it solutions like that rarely work. Unless the problem in the marriage has been the lack of a baby or the lack of a beautiful house, new home and new child will not put a marriage back together again.

The Donahues' reconciliation simply didn't work. Marge and the kids returned to New Mexico and her family, and Phil remained behind.

He took the divorce no better than he had taken the separation. His mother reports that he was traumatized. Phil began seeing a psychiatrist. "I almost went crazy," he says.

His life, after all, had been turned upside down, and he was now facing the problems that many divorced men face. Should he remain in his home in the suburbs, or should he move into an apartment? Should he throw himself into the dating scene, or should he do nothing for a while? Where should he live, how should he live?

He was, after all, a homebody, someone who used to go out with his sons and his neighbors and their kids for a game of softball or touch football or volleyball. Volleyball is not a game for a solitary man. Maybe everyone was getting divorced, but he had never thought, according to friends, that it would happen to him. And he did not glide through it. There are reports from those days, that at the mention of the word "divorce," he would freeze.

As for his social life, when he began dating, he is remembered by some as a bit hesitant and shy. He was certainly, by all accounts, not a man to rush out and purchase impressive new furniture for some chrome-and-

glass bachelor flat in a modern new building, all the
while dreaming of seductions of beautiful women and
lost time. He says as much himself.

"I don't think you can take a forty-year-old father of
five and put him in a Chicago high-rise and tell him to
go out and play," he says. "That would be the fantasy
of some unhappily married men, but I don't think it
could translate into reality. I think most forty-year-old
males who are suddenly paying child support and alimony and walk out into the candy-store world with the
attitude, 'Bring on the broads' are remarried within the
year."

"Bring on the broads" never seems to have been Phil
Donahue's attitude. Rather, it seems to have been, "What
are these women, these days, all about?"

He proceeded with curiosity, dating first a stewardess,
then, for a period of months, seeing a reporter from the
Chicago Tribune.

But according to one report, Phil Donahue, in his
middle-aged dating days, was a lot like Phil Donahue
in his teenaged dating days—a man who wasn't going
to rush a woman into bed.

One woman he saw in his newly divorced days was
Sharon O'Hara, an associate editor of *Oui*, the men's
magazine, who appeared on his show. Five feet, four
inches tall, red-headed, bright, and funny, Sharon appeared with a Miss U.S.A. and with Dr. Phyllis Chesler,
a psychologist and feminist who has written extensively
about women.

"I have a feeling they were looking for three different
lifestyles, and that I was sort of the comic relief," laughs
Sharon. "I got twelve fan letters afterward, by the way,
and after the show I remember being in Phil's office,
thinking he was very good, very professional, very open
and candid."

Off camera, as well as on, Sharon remembers, Donahue was interested in the sort of life she was leading.

"He was real intrigued about what it was like to be
a woman working for a man's magazine," she says. "I
think he also had the attitude that since he was recently
divorced and I was single, 'Oh well, we're all in the
same boat.'"

They went to supper and went dancing a few times.
It was not a serious thing, says Sharon; she never slept
with him. But though they only dated a few times, they
did talk about serious things; and Sharon—like Kathleen
Corrigan, Phil's high school girlfriend—was left with
good feelings for him.

"He was the sort of person who you felt became a
friend. He wasn't superficial," she says. "I thought he
was a very sensitive person who was . . . 'confused' is
not the word . . . who was very *curious* about the state
of male-female relationships and looking for input from
all sides. I thought he was very honest and candid about
relationships. He talked for a while about his boys, and
I got the feeling that he was probably looking for someone to be a mother to them . . . he also talked a lot about
what it was like when he was growing up, and how he
had been faithful to his wife the whole time they were
married . . . sexually speaking, he hadn't had a lot of
experience, and I got the impression he might be afraid
of someone like me . . . and I remember him saying the
stewardess had been a real education . . ."

There was something else that impressed Sharon very
much—Phil's attitude about Marge.

"I like the fact that he did not badmouth his ex-wife,"
says Sharon. "It was my impression, from the way he
talked, that she had gotten tired of being Mrs. Phil Donahue, that the divorce was her idea, and that he wasn't
sure *why* there had been a divorce—hadn't he been a

loving, faithful husband?—but he never badmouthed her or said that women's lib broke up his marriage, which would have been typical for someone in his position to have done."

And the "romantic" Phil Donahue?

"The only time we ever kissed was when he kissed me goodbye," says Sharon. "What I remember was that it was like when you are a teenager, you know: 'Well, gee, I had a nice time,' 'Gee, I had a nice time, too,' and you end up bumping noses and it's innocent and sweet and nice."

As for one of the longer relationships in his postdivorce life—the one with *Tribune* reporter Elaine Markoutsis, which reportedly went on for about six months—it broke up when his four sons came to live with him on a permanent basis.

"He felt guilty about spending time with women," she says.

It may be that O'Hara was right—perhaps Phil did want a woman who would be a mother to his children, perhaps he did want to remarry.

If so, it wouldn't have been that difficult for him. Many men in their forties are remarried within a year or two after their divorce becomes final; many find it easier to remarry than their ex-wives do. Society, after all, is on the man's side; the forty-year-old man is not under the same cultural stigma a forty-year-old woman may face in going with a much younger person, so he can choose from women his own age, as well as those much younger. Men, as they age, are considered more desirable in this culture: they are more knowledgeable, it is assumed; they have had time to become successful in their careers; the gray hair and laugh lines around the eyes only add to their "character" or "sophistication." But women, as they grow older, are often made to feel less desirable. Fashion ads feature twenty-three-year-old girls—often with forty-seven-year-old men; fashions themselves often seem to be designed for nineteen-year-old girls with perfect bodies, not for forty-year-old women who've had four or five children.

The divorced mother often does not have the access to the opposite sex that the divorced father has, since it is she, not he, who usually is awarded custody. In many cases, particularly if the woman is staying home with her children, it is the man who has the job that allows him to travel and gives him access to people, rather than the woman.

Marge Donahue was an attractive woman. She had kept her slim figure throughout her marriage; she was bright, well-read, creative, interesting.

Yet, if anyone were to have taken bets, he might have laid odds that Phil would marry first. He was, after all, the star, the celebrity in that relationship; he was, with his show, meeting any number of people.

But it was Marge who stunned everyone by remarrying first—and so quickly that her family was a bit concerned, maybe even a little shocked.

Marge's romance happened, or began to happen, as she was waiting for her divorce papers.

As someone close to Marge tells it, Marge was home, thinking about what to do with her life, when an old classmate called from St. Mary's High School. The fifteen-year reunion was coming up, the classmate said, and would Marge help out on the calling committee?

Class reunions are funny things; they conjure up old memories, bring back old dreams, sometimes force a person to recall the person he would have liked to be, or wonder if he really made the right decision in marrying this person, choosing this field. They bring back old friendships and old hurts. They bring back memories of the person he used to be—and that's a person some people would just as soon forget. Many people, faced with an invitation to a class reunion, crumple it up and forget it. But Marge obviously wasn't that sort. She told her friend she'd be glad to help out.

She got her list and began calling. There were people on the list she'd been close to, and some she knew not so well. Leon Che had been one of the latter, but they did know each other well enough to chat.

"How is it with you?" Leon asked, and Marge told him she was waiting for her divorce papers, and a bit about the kids and Dayton and Phil.

Then she asked him about his life, and he told her about his son and daughter, and about how he had lost his wife to cancer just last year.

They had coffee. They talked some more. Leon, it turned out, was an automotive engineer, a self-made man who'd built up his own business, modifying car engines, souping up cars. He was dark and attractive—"the antithesis of Phil Donahue's image," says someone who knows them both—with a large, drooping mustache. Now a woman who was concerned with status, and had been married to a television star and cared about the attention of waiters when she walked into a fancy restaurant, might never have given Leon Che, a mechanic, another look. But Marge had never cared that much for being the wife of a celebrity; to her, that sort of status was bothersome business. She liked Leon Che. She was interested.

She became more and more interested. Less than six months later—about four months after the divorce came through—she became Mrs. Leon Che.

Her family was reportedly a little concerned.

"The feeling was, 'My God, Marge, you've just disengaged, the whole world was open to you,'" says a relative.

But Marge had a very down-to-earth reply. She said, "What most people don't understand is that when a divorce becomes final, it doesn't mean the relationship has come apart simultaneously. The relationship ends many months, many years, before the divorce is final."

Is the former Mrs. Donahue content with her new life? A member of Marge's family describes the marriage as "ecstatically happy."

"Now Marge has companionship, she has a warm personal relationship," he says. "Leon is bright, not what you'd call erudite, but he can engage in conversation on any level; if you put Leon Che on Donahue's show, he could hold his own. He's a totally masculine, powerfully built man. When we went down to visit them, he picked up my youngest child with his thumbs. He's a self-made man; he enjoys the fact that he's on top of his game; he's proud of the business he's created."

He is also a man interested in pursuing his education. Last year he took his master's degree. And Marge, who went back to college after her marriage to Donahue ended, graduated with him.

Yet if Marge was happy in her marriage, her sons reportedly were not—and therein is the story of how Phil came to have custody of his boys.

It's not an episode Phil speaks of openly. When a reporter for *Good Housekeeping* asked him, in 1977, how his custody arrangement came about (in a story called "Bachelor Father"), he was vague.

"It was what I'd been praying for from the moment our marriage broke up three years ago," he said. "My biggest panic then was the prospect of life without the kids. You can't just take a father of five out of his home, stick him in a high-rise, and expect him to be happy. I really need the kids, probably more than they need me."

But exactly how did the custody arrangement come about?

A source close to both Marge and Phil at that time says the reason has to do with the boys' preference for the way they could live with Phil, as opposed to the way they were living with their mother's new husband.

"Marge's new husband comes from a Spanish-American background, and the father, in numerous families of that background, has the last word," he says. "Margie's new household had rules, it was quite different; Leon's attitude was 'this is the way it is and this is the way it will be,' and this was perceived to be unreasonable by the boys. One by one, they went back to Phil. Mary Rose, who is a soft, dainty, gentle girl, stayed with her mother and Leon."

The boys returned to a house that was different from the one they had just come from, and different from their old home—a house where, together with their father, they devised new rules, learned to set up a household.

It would be a new world for the Donahue boys. But it would be as nothing compared to the new world it would be for Phil Donahue.

CHAPTER NINE:

Bachelor Father

I have this dream that I'm enchanting the world
while my kids are at home smoking grass . . . I go
on a week's trip and take two of them along. It
halves my worry.

—Phil Donahue,
Washington Post, February 2, 1978

In the beginning of the women's movement, a joke used
to go around, a woman's joke, used by mothers and
career women alike: "Aaah," it went, "I wish *I* had a
wife."

Why not? To have a traditional wife in the traditional
marriage was, in certain selfish ways, delightful. You
have a job, and stimulating outside interests; when you
come home, the unpleasant and tedious housework has
been done and a meal is waiting. You have emotional
comfort and companionship. There is someone to ask
you about your day, take your side against the boss. And
as for children—well, if you cannot be among the very
rich, who need see their children only when they choose
to see them, while entrusting their care to someone else—
you might as well be a traditional father. For, as a traditional father, you do not have to contend with three

kids battling all afternoon, after school; you do not have the wearying questions of toddlers and the antagonism of teens. You see your children for a few hours daily, when their company does not have time to get that wearing (after all, you've had the talk of adults all day). And if a child yells for water after it's been sent off to bed, or throws up, you—as a traditional father—do not set off at a dead run to take care of your child. You yell for your traditional wife.

Phil Donahue, according to friends, and according to his mother, had not been the worst sort of traditional father—he *was* a diaper changer, after all.

And he was a man who did make attempts to be close to his children. Back in Dayton, when the family was still all together, his former secretary recalls that Phil interrupted a conversation with Ralph Nader (a hero of his) to take a phone call from his youngest son, Jimmy. Whatever the pressures or prestige of the show, his secretary says, he always made time for his children.

But according to his standards, he had been an absentee father throughout his marriage. "I was the kind of sleepwalking father who hadn't much more to offer the kids when I got home at night than an affectionate pat on the head and an absentminded 'That's nice, son,'" he said, after he'd had custody of his sons for two years, and could see the change in himself.

That "pat-on-the-head" level of parenting has very little to do with parenting on a day-to-day basis. The father who only has time to pat a kid on the head—or bawl him out if his wife suggests it—is not often in a position to get to know his children as individuals. Sure, he may notice that one son has his wife's eyes while another has his own athletic abilities, or that one child is quieter than another, or even that one is better than the others in school (an insight that usually comes when he takes a quick look at the report cards piled up on the table). But the nuances of parenting—the sensitivity to one child's vulnerabilities or strengths—are unknown to the absentee father. Much of what that father knows about his children comes, in fact, not from a firsthand knowledge of his kids, but what a man's wife tells him. No wonder, then, that, left alone with the kids, traditional fathers—and their offspring—feel awkward and uncomfortable.

Phil Donahue was not as ignorant of parenting as many absentee fathers might have been; his show saw to that. For years, he'd heard experts—and parents—discussing how to raise children; whether divorce was good or bad for a child, if the parents had been battling; when to discipline, when *not* to discipline; various methods of custody in the case of a broken marriage.

Now, suddenly, he would be playing the role of mother and father, a role that would bring him closer than anything else in his life to the world of his housewife-viewer. It would be an interesting time for Phil, for it is one thing, as an outsider, to be sympathetic to, for instance, a housewife whose neighbors are angry at her for not taking her turn at chauffering all the kids around in the neighborhood car pool—and it is quite another to be the outcast housewife yourself. Phil, in taking on single parenting, was taking on those problems. He would also learn to run a washing machine, to start thinking of the home as his responsibility, to worry if his sons' underwear was turning an unsightly gray. A year or two into single parenting, and he became quite the little housewife indeed.

"I have already noticed your socks," he told a young man in the front row of the Parent Council of Washington, when they invited him to speak there one night, then added to the rest of the crowd, "and if you invited me into your homes, I would notice your floors."

After having the boys around, Phil Donahue could
have written a treatise on socks: how to bleach them,
how *not* to bleach them, how to keep yours separate
from your sons'. (Phil's technique, which would have
put more traditional housewives into a state of shock,
was to simply write 'Dad' on his socks with a laundry
pen.)

But it would be more than socks that would pose
problems for Phil in those early days of being a bachelor
father.

One of the earliest and most serious problems he had
to deal with was finding a housekeeper. In doing that,
he did not have the problem that many single parents
have—a shortage of funds. But he was asking a housekeeper to come in and deal with four teenaged boys, to
walk that fine line between concern and substitute moth-
ering. Like anyone taking on a housekeeper or live-in
babysitter, he had to find someone who could be en-
trusted with a very responsible position. A dope fiend,
a racist, or someone with beliefs counter to his own
would not do. The perfect housekeeper had to set a good
example, and be understanding, competent, and kind.
It was not at all easy to find the right person. "Finding
good household help is one of the toughest problems of
the working single parent," said Phil. "Most of the housekeepers I've hired didn't seem to be too sympathetic to
teenage boys . . ."

"You get a housekeeper," he says, "and in three days
you have a surrogate mother. You know—the kids
should do this, they should do that. I'll say, 'Mrs. Such-
and-Such, don't go up there.' 'Well, I know it's up
there,' she'll say. I say, 'Okay, I'll talk to him.' With
a single housekeeper, it's almost like I had another
child."

Phil finally found his solution—after going through any number of housekeepers—by hiring a live-in Yugoslav couple. ("She speaks very good English. I do charades with him.")

Another problem Phil had to contend with was the feeling any working parent has to face, and that the single parent is particularly subject to: guilt.

Phil Donahue knew a lot about guilt from hearing his television guests discuss it. He'd spoken with working women who felt guilty about leaving husband and children to go to their jobs, and he'd also seen the anger of women in the audience when one of his guests was a working mother—the resentment some of the women who stayed at home with their children seemed to feel toward the working mothers. He'd heard all the words from mothers who spoke yearningly of their need for their own "space," their own "fulfillment." He'd heard all the arguments about "qualitative time versus quantitative time."

Yet he was a man, according to friends, who was prone to guilt. And his career was an area in which it was easy for him to feel guilty. He said repeatedly that his devotion to his work had hurt his marriage. Possibly he did not want to repeat that mistake as a bachelor father, bringing up his children. It would be that feeling, along with his incessant worrying ("The Irish are pretty much doom and gloom," he jokes. "You know, they make a plane and the Irish say, 'When will it crash?'"), that would often cause him to take his children with him on his frequent out-of-town trips. It would also be his concern about being a good father that would prevent him from being a hot-shot celebrity, out on the town till all hours of the night.

"I don't do the downtown thing," he says. "I'd like to, like anybody else, but I can't very well go to Detroit for a week in May on remotes, and then be home a night and do Sweetwaters (a popular local nightspot). My guilt wheel would not allow me."

His commitment is to be respected. For while the money, when one is a celebrity, may make it a little easier to be a single parent, success can also provide temptations that parents in more mundane jobs never face.

Few housewives—or single mothers or fathers—have the stack of invitations a successful show business personality receives. Few have the opportunity to travel. Many parents, particularly women who haven't had careers, express a need to "find their own identity." The successful show-business parent may have exactly the opposite problem: they have a public identity, but that identity, and the fame that goes with it, are sometimes an imposition on their children and spouse.

Phil Donahue had already seen the strain his celebrity had put on his ex-wife; Marge had had to endure flirtatious women at private parties, intrusive fans at dinners out, and constant attention paid to her husband at business functions. He was aware that scenes where he was adored while she was ignored couldn't be much fun for her, though, in his fantasy of success in his early days, he had naively thought that his success would provide his family, as well as himself, with pleasure.

"I had always pictured that one day I would be successful and that my kids would grow up to be proud," he says. "We'd all go to banquets where I would be honored and my wife would stand there like Nancy Reagan, smiling up at me like she had broken ankles."

Such was Phil's concern over the right and wrong way to handle celebrity in personal relationships, that in an appearance on "The David Susskind Show," with talk-show hosts Dick Cavett and Stanley Siegel, he put the question to Cavett.

"How do you do in the company of your celebrity wife on the difference of recognition?" he asked Cavett, who is married to actress Carrie Nye. "How do you feel when someone says hello to her and perhaps ignores you? Or how often does that happen? Obviously you have more visibility than she."

Cavett's answer was witty, as Cavett's answers usually are. But it was also frank, and did acknowledge the possible pain that could occur if one was never in the limelight, while one's spouse was.

"I like it [when she's complimented]," he said, "because I feel she's getting complimented on what is a harder thing to do than what I do. I hate to admit that, that she does a harder thing better than I do . . . but I must admit that if it went on and on, and I didn't do the show and she suddenly went against her grain and made a lot of commercial movies and nobody recognized me anymore, it would become a problem and I would probably take to drink."

The constant attention paid to one's spouse can be a strain even to a mature adult, but consider what effects having a celebrity parent can have on a child. On one hand, there may be the benefit of knowing one's parent is loved and respected by others, and the status among schoolmates that comes when one's father is a big shot.

On the other hand, there may be those nagging doubts: do the other kids like me just because I have a famous father? There is the constant intrusion of reporters and photographers asking a child to pose with Dad, smile at Dad, throw the ball to Dad. There may be feelings of resentment: why does *his* famous career have to impinge on *my* life?

"The boys don't like my being a local celebrity," said Phil. "The three older ones especially find it all embarrassing—the interviews and pictures and all. It *is* sort of an invasion of their privacy. I can understand that. One of them told me a while back he wished I wouldn't show up at Little League games because the other kids razzed him about his quote bigshot father unquote. So I don't."

Recognizing his sons' sensitivity to his celebrity was only a small part of Phil's learning about his children. He also had to learn each child's requirements in regard to privacy and discipline, and how each could best be reached. He worked at it, taking the job of parent seriously—and he was amazed at how little he had known of parenting. How easy it was to do wrong, while having the best intentions.

"When I think of how ill-equipped I was to raise kids, it scares me," he says. "Nobody ever told me how important it was to recognize children, to praise them when they did good things. Nobody ever told me that relentless criticism from a parent can really hurt a child. I felt that all I owed my kids were gifts at Christmas and an occasional spanking.

"All of us, men and women, haven't been taught to appreciate our own values. It's not anybody's fault, it's not done with malice. But children live in a world of adults who point accusatory fingers, saying, 'How could you . . . ?' 'Why did you . . . ?' 'Why didn't you . . . ?' And by the time children, especially girls, get to school, more often than not, they don't like themselves."

Phil did not want his children to grow up not liking themselves. But how to be the right mix of permissiveness and restraint, that was the problem. His former brother-in-law, Jim Cooney, might have found Phil permissive when he and Marge were together. But Phil had had the experience of going to a parochial school where boys were frequently slapped around, and it is unlikely that he wanted his own sons to grow up in such an environment. So he does raise his sons with a certain number of rules.

"I'm not Mr. Liberal," he has said, "and I don't let them do whatever they want. I scream and yell."

But he is also flexible, and has consideration for their individual likes and dislikes.

"It happens that my four would all rather jump into a pit of rattlesnakes than do anything around the house, like mowing or weeding the borders," he confided to *Good Housekeeping* magazine. "So I made a deal with them. As long as they have after-school jobs, I'll pay a gardener, even though I feel a little silly about it, but as soon as one of them doesn't, he's the gardener."

Phil also tries not to pass on to his children (daughter Mary Rose lives with him in the summer) the problems he had in growing up.

A feminist, he is particularly sensitive to put-downs regarding women, even those which may not be genuine put-downs, merely a habit of speech. The Donahue son who slips and uses the word "chick" for a girl, will often find himself on the receiving end of a short lecture.

"A chick is a helpless bird," Phil says.

When his daughter stays with him, he takes care that she doesn't see her future only in terms of marriage and family.

"In the fifties, when I went away to college, this grab-him-before-he-gets-away attitude caused a lot of going steady and a lot of early marriages," he says. "Many young women ended up in bad marriages that lasted two or three years, and some, unfortunately, which lasted a lifetime. A lifetime of misery."

For his own daughter, now fourteen, he hopes things will be different.

"She's not going to be so focused on getting married," he says. "At eighteen, marriage was just around the corner for women of previous generations. The exception was the woman who got married in her late twenties . . . also, my daughter will make more money than her mother did at the same age, and not because of inflation. The world she steps into as an adult will be more conscious of her as a human being than they were of her mother."

Sex education, when Phil was growing up, was usually unheard-of in the American school system. Much of Phil's own sex education came from lectures from school priests, telling the boys what *not* to do. Phil has often said that this preoccupation with sex-as-sin distracted boys from being able to relate well to girls, or to see girls as friends. "Concern about sex so distracted us that we failed to share ideas about more important topics," he says.

He is trying to raise his sons in an atmosphere where sex is not regarded as sin, or as a taboo subject.

"I've given them sex lectures. I drew the ovaries and the fallopian tubes. The next morning, I saw the paper, and it looked liked a psychotic had been drawing on it. You could see the tension. I'm as awkward as any parent when it comes to talking about sex," he says.

He's trying, however. He's assuming the role of mother and father, from developing theories on an adolescent's need for privacy (each of his sons has his own room), to learning about such mundane tasks as shopping for teenagers.

Exhaustion is not really understood until one has spent the day with a fourteen-year-old, covering every store in town, hearing moans of 'I'm too skinny,' 'I'm too fat,' or, 'Mother, puh-*lease.*' How many fathers do you see, the week before school begins, taking the kids shopping?

Yet Phil—having gone through the struggle of finding a housekeeper, having tackled the mysteries of washing machines and dryers and bleach—went gamely into that strange new world of children's clothing.

"I was never aware of the frustration of buying teenagers clothes," he says. "They're all too baggy or too tight or too low, or they're high-waisted and they won't wear those. And girls' clothes—girls are even worse. They said, 'Is she preteen?' I said, 'She's eleven.' They said, 'But is she *preteen?*' "

His confusion was to be expected; how was Phil to know that 'preteen' was a size as well as an age? He was also enlightened about half-sizes, misses' sizes, junior sizes. He was not pleased.

"Who invented this system?" he asked a shopper.

"A man," she said.

Still, he feels that the experience has been illuminating.

"Being a single parent is an opportunity," he says, "not a pain in the neck. My consciousness has been raised. I'm a very fortunate fellow . . . there are those men who are reduced to visiting their kids on weekends when a child may have other things to do and can't because Dad is coming to visit, and Dad then becomes a concentrated father, a Disneyland Dad . . . you have just a weekend . . . I'm very grateful I'm not reduced to that."

Being a single parent, spending more time with his kids, Phil has also developed some thoughts on the right and wrong ways to raise children.

"I think, too often, mothers and fathers tend to see

parenting as a sort of martyrdom," he says. "They're always getting the message across to their kids in one way or another: 'See what a pain in the neck you are?' 'See how much I have to do for you?' I think the most important thing we can do for our kids is to let 'em know we're glad to have them, let 'em feel happy, instead of guilty, about being kids.

"People used to say to me, 'You have great kids,' and I'd say, 'Yeah, if only they'd do their homework,' or, 'Sure, if only they'd put gas in the car.' I used to push, pull, prod them, trying to mold them as though they were pieces of clay. I'd ask why they didn't change their shirts or wear a belt or develop an interest in something *I* wanted them to be interested in. But living closely with them has taught me that they're people in their own right, and now I want them to be what *they* want to be. Now, when people praise the kids, I say, 'Yeah, you're absolutely right.' And I tell the kids how great they are every chance I get."

In the years following the divorce, Phil tried to enjoy his children. He tried to be with them as often as possible; he did not spend night after night out on the town. The situation, as it will with a single parent, put a crimp in his dating habits. (Though all indications are that Phil would not have been very happy as a playboy.)

Still, something was missing. Phil had his sons, he had a family—but for a long period of time, there was no serious woman in his life. For a man who enjoyed the company of women, it was an ironic situation. But it was not going to last forever.

CHAPTER TEN:

Marlo

You are loving and generous and wonderful, and whoever is the woman in your life is lucky.

> —Marlo Thomas to Phil, on his television show

When it happened, and the word got back to his old friends in Dayton, more than a few would comment that this new woman in Phil's life, with her dark eyes, high cheekbones, and tall, slim body, looked amazingly like his ex-wife.

When it happened, his new friends would not be surprised, for hadn't Marlo Thomas, on Phil's show, admitted that she was "depressed" when there wasn't a man in her life, and wasn't Phil Donahue a family man who needed a serious relationship?

When it happened, people who did not really know either of them had their doubts—what could the son of a furniture salesman from Cleveland, Ohio, possibly have in common with the daughter of one of the wealthiest comedians in the country? What could a woman who had always been a career woman, and always been single, have to say to a man who had been married most of his adult life?

But the people who said that were wrong. For while, on the surface, Marlo and Phil might have seemed miles apart—she growing up in a Beverly Hills mansion, he waiting tables in college—they actually had a great many things in common. Both were from religious Catholic families. Both had proud, doting parents. Both were the oldest children in their families. (Psychologists say that oldest sons and daughters often are ambitious, responsible, and highly motivated.) Both grew up with a strong sense of social responsibility. Both came from homes in which their parents played the traditional male-female roles. ("My mother was in the kitchen, Dad on the stage; it was all very clear-cut," says Marlo.) And both had instinctively sought out the stage—over their parents' objections. True, Marlo's childhood was radically different from Phil's; she grew up in the sophisticated world of Hollywood, living in a household where the people Phil heard on the radio or saw on television—Fanny Brice, Milton Berle, Sid Caesar, and Frank Sinatra (a close friend of Danny Thomas), came as guests to dinner.

Yet Marlo had also grown up aware of her father's struggle and sacrifice. For, when Marlo was born, Danny, who had not yet made it, was a struggling Detroit comic, earning thirty-five dollars a week. Success would come for him within a few years of Marlo's birth, and Marlo's early years, like Phil's, were spent in an extremely religious household. The lawn behind her father's fine mansion was dominated by a statue of St. Jude, the patron saint of the hopeless; a wood carving of the Last Supper dominated the living room; prayer was practiced and encouraged. In fact, Danny Thomas believed that prayer and faith had helped him to achieve success. Back in the early days, struggling to make it as a comic, out of work, just married, with a baby on the way, down to his last seven dollars, he had knelt before a statue of St. Jude and asked for help. "Should I stay in show business?" he had asked. "Do I belong? If I do stick it out and make good, I'll build a shrine."

Thomas did make good. A few years after Marlo's birth, he was making $3500 a week as a comic in Chicago and New York. And he did follow through on his promise to St. Jude, raising millions of dollars for the St. Jude Hospital in Memphis, Tennessee, a hospital specializing in the treatment of children's diseases.

But the memory of her father's sense of obligation to others, and of his answered prayers, is one of the things, says Marlo, that has made her the woman she is today; it gave her the feeling that it is important to reach out, to be of service—a feeling Donahue shares.

"I don't consider what I'm doing that noble or special, because most of the people I know are involved in helping others," she said once, at a time when she was involved with feminist projects. "It's sort of part of life, it seems. And we all need it. I mean, I need to be encouraged and inspired as much as anyone else, and I think we all give nutrition to each other that way. But I was raised in a family that was particularly like that; since I was a little girl, my father was building St. Jude Hospital. And I can remember, when I was five years old, that he had a painting of what the hospital was going to look like, and he was raising money on that painting. They didn't even have the land yet, but he knew what he wanted to build. And we had a motto in our family that hung in the dining room, that was on a wooden plaque. My father had been knighted by the Pope, so we were presented with a family crest. We had to have a motto for the crest, so my father chose, 'Blessed are they who know why they are born.' He always felt that the reason he was born was to build that hospital. So you're raised in that kind of climate."

From the time she was a little girl, Marlo wanted to be an actress. When she was six, she used to curtain off one end of a big walk-in closet, and burst out from behind the curtain, singing, "Toot-toot-tootsie, good-bye . . ."

"We went to nightclubs to see my father work, then we'd come home and imitate," she says. "I remember, when I was very little, I had visions of dancing in a chorus line, one of the short girls. I'd be 'Chez Paree Adorable,' a high-kicking chorus girl. I wanted something I could own, a success I could lay claim to, but I grew up knowing my father's career went up and down."

Marlo knew, in short, what Phil's father had known: show business was a risky life that did not offer financial or emotional security. In fact, had Phil's father and Marlo's father ever met, they might have agreed on many things.

"My father didn't want me to become an actress," says Marlo. "He was always bugging me about it because—as he later told me—he didn't want to relive his own terrible starting years with someone he loved. Those are the weeding-out years, you know, when so many girls decide to go back to the farm or wherever they came from, rather than face another frustrating rejection by a producer or a director or a sponsor. No matter who a girl's father may be, when she's out there in front of the lights, she's all alone."

Marlo, like Phil, opted in college for a secure future. At the University of California, she studied to be an English teacher—even though, like Phil, she spent a lot of time at college in school drama productions.

"When I was growing up, legitimacy was the big thing," she says. "A teaching certificate gave me that.

I was qualified. I could do something even if I didn't make it in show business."

Like Phil, however, Marlo's plans for a secure career did not last beyond college. Just after graduation, she starred in a Pasadena Playhouse production of *Gigi*. It was a role that, in her case, brought with it some special pressures.

"The papers took the attitude, 'Let's see what the young Thomas is like, what Danny's daughter has to offer,'" she says. "I talked to my father about it, and he pointed out that in life you have to run your own race. He said thoroughbreds don't watch what the other horses are doing. You put blinders on and run your own race."

It was advice Marlo would remember, and advice her father wanted her to remember. On opening night, in her dressing room, along with the opening-night telegrams and flowers, Marlo received a package containing a pair of horse blinders and a note. "Run your own race, baby. Love, Daddy," it said.

And after the play—a performance that may have meant as much to Marlo as Phil's role in *Death of a Salesman* meant to him—her father came backstage and gave her new career his blessings.

"That was the part that won my father over," says Marlo, smiling at the memory. "He came backstage and said to me that I really belonged in the theater. By that time, I had already convinced myself that I should try to achieve something on my own as an actress. I wasn't going to be stopped in that ambition, of course, but I still felt relieved that my father would no longer object. I love him very much, and I would much rather be in accord with him than not."

Marlo set out to make a career for herself. In doing

so, however, it was with the awareness that she might well be making a choice between the stage and marriage. That choice had nothing to do with her feelings toward men; it had more to do with the times. Marlo had been born in 1938; she was of the same generation as Donahue, and she had been raised when there was a feeling that one could simply not be a mother and a wife *and* a career woman. Marlo also seemed to feel that marriage meant sacrificing her own needs in order to sustain and nurture a man—an attitude that may have come from watching her mother, a one-time radio singer, give up her career to build her life around Danny Thomas. Perhaps her mixed feelings about combining marriage and career also came out of seeing how little time a successful entertainer has for his family—despite his best efforts.

"My father had to work really hard to be a good father," said Marlo once. "He was easily a good person . . . and a loving person . . . but he traveled so much, and his work was so demanding, it was very hard for him to give to the family what he felt was necessary . . . but he did it."

That traveling often took both Marlo's mother and father away.

"Miss Independence, that was my nickname," says Marlo. "Maybe it's because I was the eldest and I was the mommy so often. When I was growing up, Mother and Daddy traveled a lot. Mother had a way of talking to us so we never felt like kiddies. One day we were all crying because she was going away again. She said, 'Daddy is working away from home. Now there are three of us girls (Marlo, her mother, and her younger sister), and if Daddy doesn't have a girl, he'll have to get one. So one of us has to go, and you're going off to school.' Mother really made us feel 'poor Daddy.'"

Marlo's big break came when Mike Nichols asked her to audition for the Broadway production of *Barefoot in the Park* (Elizabeth Ashley, the show's star, was leaving). As it happened, however, Ashley's understudy had been promised that role without Nichols's knowledge, so he offered Marlo the lead in the touring company. With no small amount of trepidation, she declined.

"I've been there," she said sweetly. Nichols later asked her to star in the show in London. She did, and she scored.

"A great new comic actress," raved one critic. "A shapely doll ... who scorches the stage with a performance that leaves you breathless," said another. Those reviews meant a lot to Marlo, for they came in a country where she was judged for herself, not as Danny Thomas's daughter. She stayed in the role for eight months, then came back to the United States for a role that would make her a star in her own country—that of a struggling actress in the TV sitcom "That Girl."

She didn't take the part because she was hard-pressed for cash: "I'd be lying if I said I didn't have my own trust fund and could always dip into it. My father's a very wealthy man," she told gossip columnist Earl Wilson, as she began work on her television series.

No, what motivated Marlo in her work wasn't a need for money. It was a feeling that she was happiest on stage. In fact, while some of Phil's close friends had said that he seemed at his happiest when performing, that his desire for the spotlight was possibly a *need* for the spotlight, the same might be said of Marlo.

"All my life I've been starving, while feasting for twenty-five years on the best of everything," Marlo said at the time of her series, to New York *Daily News* reporter Kay Gardella. "There's more than one way of being hungry. In my case, I find the one thing that fulfills me is acting. It's the only time I'm truly happy and no matter how many sacrifices I have to make to become a star, it's all right with me.

"I'm not worried about hard work," Marlo continued. "I have tremendous drive. I'm very hard on myself. I really can't stand to be second best. When we made the pilot film for "That Girl," I blew three comedy lines that should have gotten laughs, but didn't, the way I read them. While it was true that very few people would notice it, what's important is that *I* did know it. Even when I was complimented on my performance in the pilot episode, all I could think of were those three lousy lines."

That drive, that need for perfection, that tendency to be very hard on herself, were things that Marlo would one day share with Phil. And there would be something else she would share with Phil: a tendency to be considered too demanding—even a reputation, in some quarters, for being unpleasant. "Bitchy" is the word that crops up here and there. But that so-called bitchiness was a by-product, perhaps, of Marlo's inexhaustible energy, or perhaps her tendency to push everyone as hard as she pushed herself.

"I think there's a lot of hours in a day, a lot of living to be done. I'm not a good spectator. I want to be in it. I want to die from being tired, not from being sick and bored. God gave me every opportunity to live," she said early in her career.

And as her career progressed, her drive did not diminish. On the set of "That Girl," in its early days, she worked to such an extent that the director himself finally told her to cool it.

"In the first year of 'That Girl,' you can imagine what I was like with my own television series," she said. "And in my twenties. My first chance. My God, I was like a maniac, running around, trying to do everything. And the director said to me, after a couple of weeks had gone by, 'What is it with you? Every shot is opening night?' And I was startled. I said, 'Yes.' Well, yes! Isn't it? I mean if it isn't, what is this? Of course every shot is opening night. And every shot in everything is. Or else why are you doing it? You don't want it to be boring.''

She acknowledges that such a viewpoint may make the people around you hostile or irritated.

"I'm sure they look at you and say you're a pain in the ass," she says. "The people who have to backtrack because you've changed your mind and actually improved something, to make it better for everybody, they'll be mad at you. They'll say, 'What does it matter?'"

It can work two ways with the children of famous parents: they can give up, feeling overwhelmed by their parent's reputation; or they can work very hard to strike out on their own—perhaps motivated by their parent's stardom, by a need to be their own person.

"I want very much to be my own person, especially in the light of my having a great father," she told a *New York Post* reporter, back in her early days. "You have a chance to be a human being, but for that you must assert your own identity. We [she and her brother and sister] were encouraged to spread out; some children of famous parents are overshadowed from the beginning. They become reticent and babbling."

It was extremely important for Marlo to assert her independence. And, interestingly enough, the character of "That Girl"—the actress who comes to New York to strike out on her own—was a girl whose story was much like Marlo's (except that the heroine of "That Girl" is called Ann Marie, and her father was a restaurant owner in Brewster, New York, rather than a famous comedian).

True, Marlo Thomas was not absolutely independent of her famous father—"That Girl" was written by Bill Persky and Sam Denoff, two of Danny Thomas's most successful writers (they had written "The Dick Van Dyke Show," which Thomas had produced). And at one point, reports had it, Thomas himself had been thinking of doing a show very similar to "That Girl" called "Miss Independence" (Marlo's childhood nickname).

But Marlo worked very hard to be successful in her TV show—and in control. Her own company, Daisy Productions, produced the show, giving her a bit more independence than an actress usually gets. If it was shooting exteriors in the streets of New York, where "That Girl" was set, or working back in Hollywood, where most of the show was really shot, Marlo was on the set on time, ready to go. And her efforts paid off. The day after the show debuted, there were raves.

"Marlo Thomas is a charmer," gushed one New York television writer. "That's why her situation comedy . . . is a delight. The first playlet, in itself, about a girl who works as a candy counter aide in New York while trying to become an actress was no better than many other programs in this category; but what made it click was the completely endearing and humor-filled performance of this daughter of comedian Danny Thomas . . . Marlo Thomas has made it on her own. And Daddy had better watch out. He may soon be known as the father of a famous daughter."

Said *Look* magazine, as the show, an acknowledged hit, went into its second season: "Television series are comic books that you don't have to read. Week after week after week, hundreds of glazed Americans sit around watching their favorite cast of characters leap mini-hurdle after mini-hurdle, which they conquer in an endless variety of ways. The best that can be said for these cartoons set to electronics is that occasionally a player comes along who is so pleasant or amusing or interesting (rare) that being in his or her company is almost worth the idiocy of the show. Such a one is the star of ABC's "That Girl," saucer-eyed, furry-eyelashed Marlo Thomas. Marlo plays a sort of dippy, would-be actress whose fever-pitch enthusiasm makes Mary Poppins look as if she had tired blood."

True, the acclaim would not be universal. Just as Phil would have his detractors, Marlo had hers. That cutsey-pie, perky, relentlessly cheerful actress she played on "That Girl" certainly did get on some people's nerves; one critic went so far as to suggest meanly that with Marlo, some California kids had found a substitute for LSD—that they turned the sound off their TV's, and amused themselves by watching Marlo change her expression fifty times a minute. (Phil Donahue is also sometimes criticized for a too-innocent, too-wholesome TV persona.)

As for Marlo's father, while Danny Thomas would be proud of his daughter's success, and say she was "an original," Danny would still say that, in his heart, he had some ambivalent feelings about Marlo in show business.

"I don't know. If she were a boy, I'd be jumping up and down," said Danny, at the time of Marlo's triumph. "I'd have a son in the business. This way, well, we're old-fashioned—what I wish she'd do is get married and have another Marlo."

Danny seemed destined for disappointment. "That Girl" ran five years, and when it stopped, that was Marlo's decision. "I just thought it was time for all of us to move on to something else," she said at the time. And while Marlo had her long-run relationships—for, like Phil, she was not one to gravitate toward short-term, flighty affairs—she did not seem interested in marriage. During "That Girl," she kept company with ABC executive Leonard Goldberg; later, she saw playwright Herb Gardner, author of *A Thousand Clowns*, for nearly five years.

With "That Girl" behind her, Marlo tried her hand at other things: films, TV specials. But it was not just show business that interested her. "That Girl" went off the air in 1971, as all sorts of things were happening in this country—the women's movement, the antiwar movement. And just as Phil was aware of the changes, so was Marlo. Neither was she a mere observer—this was, after all, the woman who said she could not bear to be a spectator. She campaigned for George McGovern in every primary, was an elected delegate to the Democratic Convention, and was active at the convention on the women's caucus.

But—as with Phil—the roles of men and women would most engage Marlo's interests. True, unlike Phil, she had grown up aware of the stereotypes, and had tried to fight them; unlike Phil, she had not allowed herself to be placed in a traditional role. She had fought for a career and independence.

Still, there are levels of awareness, degrees of outrage. Women all around her were beginning to get very angry about discrimination on the basis of sex, but part of Marlo's own consciousness-raising had to do with a subject close to home—something as seemingly insignificant as finding a bedtime story to read to her three-year-old niece.

Finding a bedtime story might seem to be an easy task—there are the classics, after all, of fairy princesses kissing frogs, and fragile princesses dreaming for a hundred years, until some strong, aggressive prince comes along and breaks the spell.

But as she looked over the old fairy tales and the modern children's books, Marlo found them offensive. Not only were many of the stories dreary, they were sexist as well.

"In the books, boys invent things and girls use them," she said. "That kind of a thing is a putdown of the human race."

Looking at those books was a reminder of the inequities of her own childhood, where the roles of little boys and little girls were defined as they had been in Phil's world.

Hers had been, after all, a world where both sets of grandparents (Lebanese on her father's side, Italian on her mother's) had had their marriages arranged for them. And in her father's family, where he had been one of nine sons, and there was one daughter, Danny Thomas and his brothers and father would eat in the dining room, while Danny's mother and his sister ate by themselves in the kitchen.

"I saw the way my mother and aunts were pushed around, the way girl children were asked to do maid's work," says Marlo. "We were asked to do cleaning up that my brother didn't have to do. We had to struggle for every privilege, such as driving and going out at night, while he got everything faster and more easily. In school, the nuns used to warn me, 'You'll need math to balance the family budget.'"

At age ten, Marlo was angry enough at the situation to write a booklet called "Women Are People Too."

At age thirty-three, in 1972, she got together a bunch of famous friends—Alan Alda, Mel Brooks, Dick Cavett, Harry Belafonte, Diana Ross, Carol Channing—to produce a record called *Free to Be . . . You and Me*.

It was not a venture for profit. Proceeds of the record went to a foundation set up by *Ms*. magazine for education programs for both women and children.

It was a venture for enlightenment, a record that was supposed to bring home the idea that boys and girls have a *choice*—that little girls did not have to necessarily be nurses while little boys could grow up to be doctors. It also stressed the importance of expressing feelings; there was none of the popular nonsense that men shouldn't cry.

"It's all right to cry/Cryin' gets the sad out of you . . ." sang no less than former football pro Rosey Grier.

Carol Channing sang a song about housework being tedious and dreary, and suggested that mommies and daddies *share* the drudge work. As for the old fairy tales, *Free to Be . . . You and Me* presented them with a new twist: the king promises his daughter's hand in marriage to the faster runner in a race, all right—but then the winner says he doesn't want to marry a woman who is being forced to marry him. Warmed by this liberated prince, the princess has a friendly talk with him—after which they go off on their separate and single lives.

The album made Marlo, in the eyes of the public, a feminist activist, even though, in certain ways, she had been a liberated woman for a long time.

"I've probably been a closet feminist all my life—but didn't know it," she said, at the time the album came out.

She was also a feminist who did not think it was so bad for a woman to put on makeup to look pretty—a feminist who, in fact, had had her nose fixed and made no secret of it. She would take a man's arm when crossing an icy street, and she enjoyed looking terrific. And if that was a problem for some people, she said it was no problem for her.

"I don't see any conflict between wanting to look your best and being liberated," she said. "Being unliberated is when you depend on your looks as your passport, the card you carry to enter the world. If it raises your self-esteem to wear makeup, wash your hair every day, and paint your nails, then you should do it, just as long as it isn't the center of your life. If I were a man, I'd steam my tie every morning, I'm sure."

She would never be among the more belligerent women of the movement, that was certain.

"If being a feminist means letting women—and children—find themselves without being confined to stereotyped roles, then I'm a feminist," she said. "If it means burning a building, I'm not."

That sort of attitude did not garner affection for her among the more militant feminists, nor did her penchant for pretty clothes.

"It's a rip-off, she's a poor little rich girl who's figured out that the movement pays," said one angry feminist. "This year she's into kids. If gladiators are the thing next year, she'll be into gladiators."

Marlo Thomas was not ignorant of the fact that a lot of feminists mistrusted her. She also knew she was considered by some as more "acceptable" a feminist than, say, the "tough" Gloria Steinem.

"Gloria is kind and caring, a real softie," she says in Steinem's defense. "If people mean she'll fight to the death for her ideals, yes, she's tough."

A whirlwind of publicity activities—that was one of the things *Free to Be . . . You and Me* brought Marlo; newspaper interviews, lectures, television talk shows. Such a spin may look glamorous to an outsider—all those strangers battling each other simply to hear what one has to say—but in fact, a publicity tour is a grueling thing. A touring author or actor may fly into town, stay for a day or two, and sometimes be booked for five or six interviews a day. Marlo did all that; she traveled, she talked, she gave interview after interview about why little boys and little girls should grow up as equals.

One of the places she hit on the talk-show circuit was the Donahue show in Dayton, Ohio—a show where many feminists, including her good friend Gloria Steinem, made frequent stops, and found their reception friendly.

Now, it would be wonderful to say it was love at first sight, that meeting just prior to airtime, the two simply knew they were meant for each other. But that, the way Marlo tells it, was not what happened. Certainly, she liked Phil well enough.

"He was wonderful, he was really a good interviewer," she says.

But there were complications. "He was married at the time and I was going out with someone and it was late at night," says Thomas, succinctly.

So Phil went home to Marge and the kids, and Marlo went back to New York and Herb Gardner—and kept stumping for the feminists.

Life for Marlo, however, was not all women's movement activities. She tried one film, *Jenny*, with Alan Alda, which was not a financial success; she had a TV special called "Acts of Love . . . and Other Comedies," that dealt with the roles men and women play. Then, in April, 1974, she found herself suddenly a Broadway star again. It was not simply to further her own career; it was also to help out her boyfriend, Herb Gardner, who had written the show—a comedy about a disintegrating contemporary marriage, called *Thieves*. Troubled from the moment the show had tried out in Boston (the producer left), the show continued to have difficulties in New York (where the leading lady left). Enter Marlo. Her boyfriend summoned her, and she came. Simple.

"I only knew I was needed," she said at the time.

"It was like being at a traffic accident. I couldn't stay away."

The notices on the show were mixed; Marlo fared somewhat better than the play itself. Still, it was successful enough to enjoy a fairly long run, and successful enough to be made into a movie—starring Marlo.

A new movie meant another round of talk shows, and once again, Marlo found herself talking with Phil Donahue, that good-looking host who had once so impressed her as an interviewer.

Why do two people fall in love? When you're very young, or very inexperienced, it's nice to think people fall in love because they get along so well, or because they are "fated" together, and because they just think the other is magnificent, from the moment they meet.

But as you get older, you realize that love is often a question of timing—of being *prepared* to love, able to appreciate someone who, in another time, you might have overlooked or ignored.

For Marlo and Phil the timing was obviously right. Certainly some very obvious things had changed in both their lives. He was no longer married, and she was not involved with Gardner the way she had been. But there were other ways in which they were right for each other. Phil, because of his dealings with the feminist movement, because of the questions he took daily from an audience of women, was now more sensitive to a woman with a career of her own. Already a family man, he did not need a woman who would give him children, though a woman who was sensitive to children was important to him. From Marlo's point of view, Phil, as a bachelor father, was particularly aware of the plight of women.

They clicked. On screen. They talked about love and marriage and careers, and they talked the way people talk when they're very excited: energetically, with animation. They interrupted each other, they laughed, they glowed—Marlo, at one point, was so enthusiastic that she playfully gave the host a little punch. (A sexual invitation, some psychologists would say, if ever there was one.) And some of the questions, it soon became clear, were being asked on behalf of the host as well as his audience.

"How important is love?" Donahue asked Thomas. (A question, one can assume, he would not have asked Ralph Nader.)

Thomas didn't dodge it.

"I like having a man in my life. I like someone to love me and I like being in love. I've had serious and loving relationships with men."

"How are you when there's no one in your life?" asked Phil.

"Depressed," said Marlo.

They were high on each other, no question, no secret.

"This is what happens when an equal woman and an equal man get together," said Marlo. And later, with eight million women hanging on every word: "You are loving and generous and wonderful, and whoever is the woman in your life is lucky."

When the show was over, they went their separate ways. But "that girl" had that show on her mind.

"It's a fabulous talk show," she says, "and he's a fabulous man. We found that we had a lot to talk about . . . marriage . . . to have children or not . . . women in the job market . . . our own backgrounds . . . We enjoyed sharing ideas with each other right away. A lot of clicks happened. He kept saying things and I would think, 'What an interesting thing to comment on' . . . We enjoyed sharing ideas with each other right away, and I left having a very nice feeling about him."

He did not, however, call Marlo that evening, or even

the next. Perhaps, from the way she tells the story, he might have needed a bit of reassurance.

"A week or so later, on another talk show, the host mentioned that Phil Donahue thought I was terrific, and I said, 'I think he's terrific.' And it wasn't long before he called me."

Neither was it long before the two were seen around town together. True, Phil Donahue was not out on the town as much as a lot of other celebrities; he was sole parent to four boys, and he usually chose to go home and have dinner with them, or spend evenings at home. But he and Marlo were seen here and there: at the Chicago Symphony; in New York with her friends; back in Chicago, often at his favorite restaurant, Chez Paul, a terrifically romantic French restaurant, housed in a 103-year-old mansion.

They hit some of the "beautiful people" places. When John Denver had his Celebrity Pro-Am Ski Classic in Aspen, there, along with Dick Smothers, Cloris Leachman, Clint Eastwood, and Steve Martin, were Phil and Marlo: he on the slopes; he and she, at night, in the discos; she in expensive fur coats; he in jeans and sport jacket.

They spent more and more time together. When Phil took his staff to Hawaii for a thank-you present, Marlo came along; at Christmastime, Marlo joined Phil and his four sons. When it was his birthday, Marlo slipped off to Chez Paul to confer with owner Bill Contos about a special menu (Phil is the sort of down-to-earth guy who likes a Heineken with his French food, after all) for his surprise party.

"She wanted to make it a supper party," recalls Contos. "Small, just thirty-five people, and the kids were naturally included. We had continuous entertainment; some Irish minstrels, then a couple of Italian guys play-

ing the accordion, then Franz Bentler and his strolling
violinists . . . twelve or fifteen of them, I'd say. For dinner we had roast stuffed veal with a chestnut dressing,
which was very beautiful, and cognac and champagne.
Marlo decorated the whole room with flowers, so it
looked like somebody's home."

A woman doesn't go to such pains or expense to make
an evening perfect unless she is very fond of a man, as
Marlo was fond of Phil. And as the women's magazines
homed in, to find out all about this modern love story,
where the principles lived 2,000 miles apart, she made
no secret of her feelings.

"He's curious to learn and to experience. It's one of
the most important qualities in a human being," she fairly
gushed to *Ladies' Home Journal.* "And he is so great
with his children . . . they are exceptional kids, all different, and you see the love they have for him and the
desire he has, the burning desire, to help them find their
way in this world, to do anything he can do to insure
their emotional passage. It's lovely to see."

Phil was likewise publicly adoring. "Marlo is part of
the American consciousness," he told a reporter. "She
is enormously respected and admired. She also just happens to be beautiful. You don't know attention until you
walk into a department store with Marlo Thomas."

Whether all that adoration would end in marriage was
hard to say. Phil's good friend, George O'Donnell,
thought not, though he couldn't say precisely why. Phil
would skirt the issue. "Let's just say we get along very
well," he'd say.

As for Marlo, it was also hard to say. But a change
in her attitude toward marriage could be detected—a
change that began even before she met Phil. At the time
of *Free to Be . . . You and Me,* she was acknowledging
that she thought two people could live together, without

loss of identity to either. And with Donahue, that point of view was strengthening.

"I never thought marriage would be possible for me," she once said. "I'm just beginning to think it might be. Shooting for the moon, maybe, but possible and a state to aspire to."

She also acknowledged that the concept of marriage had changed since the time she was a college graduate twenty years ago, and all of her friends were getting married.

"The time of getting married for status or financial security is over," she said. "Today marriage is all about feelings and finding someone to share the world with. It involves two people taking real pride in each other's accomplishments and still retaining their individuality. It's so sad to see a woman act differently just because she's around a man, just because she thinks she has to behave the way somebody else expects her to. But as long as you hang onto yourself as a person, I think marriage can work."

As for the women's movement, and the breakdown of traditional roles for men and women, she felt that it should strengthen the bonds between husband and wife, not make a marriage (or any relationship, for that matter) less romantic.

"I don't think love is really possible between un-equals," she said. "If a husband ignores his wife and leaves her in the kitchen, well, who's he going to *talk* to? Two people need that communication, which makes everything grow; your mind, your sex life . . . all of it grows from the continual flow of communication; it's all the fruit of the same tree. If men are really in search of love, then perhaps that desire will motivate them to insure women the right to be free, to be equal. Only when you have love from someone who gives it of their own will, do you know what love is."

Granted, the relationship between Marlo and Phil had its strains, what with his talk show and her career; also with him living in Chicago and her in New York or California. At times, Marlo and Phil only saw each other twice a month, though they often vacationed together (a week in the Caribbean, maybe) and usually talked together every day.

Nonetheless, these strains must have served only to reaffirm their commitment to one another because, despite their former reservations about marriage, Phil and Marlo have indeed decided to "shoot for the moon." They were wed on May 22, 1980, at Danny Thomas's home in California. Only immediate family attended the ceremony which the couple had kept so confidential that even Phil's staff found out about it from the press the following day. At the time of this writing the famous newlyweds are on an extended honeymoon in Europe.

CHAPTER ELEVEN:

Behind the Scenes at the Donahue Show

> I respect these women, but okay, some of what I do is showbiz. Don't forget there's a guy on the other channel giving away $25,000, and he's got a woman jumping up and down dressed like a chicken salad sandwich and, by God, I better have something going on my show because this is a very competitive business.
>
> —Phil Donahue,
> *New York Times*, May 20, 1979

For all the pain and upheaval and confusion of his personal life—and all the growth—the Chicago years were good years for Phil Donahue, as far as his show was concerned.

Hot in Dayton, he continued to be hot in Chicago. Arriving in Chicago in 1974, with his show syndicated in forty-five cities, by late 1977 he was viewed in 120 cities. In May of 1977, six months short of the tenth anniversary of the show, he received an Emmy Award as best host of a daytime talk or variety show. Picked up on NBC in New York (something for which the show had hoped for a long time), he was approached by that network in 1977 about the possibility of someday hosting the "Today" show. And, while both NBC and Phil denied that there had been an actual offer, Phil was quick to admit that the offer had been flattering.

"The thing that's neat about the 'Today' show is the power," he said. "If I were with 'Today' and called Cyrus Vance, he'd probably return the call. Of course, if Vance came on the show, I'd probably have a frustrating time interviewing him in six and a half minutes—and then having to go to the Alpo commercial. It would be a new challenge."

He had arrived, no question. The man who, back in Dayton, had rushed to the airport at 2:00 A.M. to meet Ralph Nader and convince him to come on the show, now could book Muhammad Ali or Lillian Carter. ("Phil, I don't wear an IUD, I'm not a homosexual, and I don't smoke pot—what am I going to talk about?" Miss Lillian teased, when he asked her to appear.)

The man who, when he had first flown into Chicago to do his show, had worried about bombing, was now getting wonderful press.

"Phil Donahue simply is the finest talk show emcee in the business," wrote *Chicago Tribune* TV critic Gary Deeb. "His daily program . . . reduces the Mervs and Mikes and Dinahs to the level of Tupperware parties. He has been the best for a long time, but the video power brokers in New York ignored him until the Emmy came along and WNBC-TV signed up his show."

Said TV critic Bill Carter, "One of the reasons it is so unfortunate to get sick and have to stay home all day in bed is daytime television. Daytime television hasn't made many sick people get better. Then again, it may have helped some marginally ill patients flee the sickroom as fast as possible."

The exception, the critic continued, was Donahue: "Instead of being just one more celebrity showcase, or one more frothy appeal to the superficial side of femininity, 'Donahue' is invariably a show with guts. It tackles serious issues squarely. It steers straight ahead into controversy without fear of repercussions, it tells its viewers they can be discriminating and demanding and get something out of television . . . Donahue also attracts the offbeat kind of guest, the kind that makes a human being think. He also puts on his share of celebrities, but usually gets beyond the Mike Douglas level of, 'How's your pet cockatoo?'"

Critics noted that when Donahue brought on the celebrities, his aggressive—yet sympathetic—questioning brought responses other interviewers failed to get. Lillian Carter, asked teasingly by Donahue whether or not she had ever "lusted in her heart," admitted that she had indeed, once or twice; Dinah Shore, normally reticent about discussing her private life—and an experienced interviewer herself—talked rather openly about how painful her breakup with Burt Reynolds had been.

The show *did* steer straight ahead into controversy. A program that featured two lesbian mothers, living together as a couple and raising their small children, brought cries of outrage and cancellations from some of the show's subscribers. A show that showed an actual abortion was cancelled by the brass at WGN in Chicago, Phil's home station. And perhaps the greatest storm was created when a Chicago couple, rather than have their baby in a hospital, opted for an at-home delivery—and invited Phil, his crew, and the television audience to be there with them. For that show, Donahue and company spent the fifteen hours during which the mother was in labor at the family's home, filming, then put together a show that included the film of the birth, followed by the couple and their doctor discussing at-home deliveries.

Once again, WGN cancelled—as did stations in

Cleveland, Nashville, St. Louis, Miami, and San Francisco.

"It was simply too graphic for that time period," said WGN's station manager Harry Trigg, at the time, "and I personally thought it was a little sensational. My feeling is that television doesn't have to be that exploitative. We felt it was far too graphic for eleven o'clock in the morning when children are watching. Also, there's nothing really that startling about natural childbirth. People have been doing it in large numbers for five or six years now. To me, the program wasn't that enlightening."

The viewers—and critics—disagreed.

Chicago Tribune critic Gary Deeb smashed the WGN management, calling the cancellation "reactionary."

A member of the television audience from Centerville, Ohio, whose local network had not cancelled the show, agreed with Deeb.

"It is far past the time for us to outgrow our secretive attitudes about birth," the viewer wrote, then went on to contrast the Donahue show with a local program she had seen on childbirth. "In a supposedly educational program on birth, 'My Mom is Having a Baby,' broadcast a few years back, it appeared as if the baby came out of sterile sheets—not much better than the proverbial 'doctor's little black bag.' A deplorable situation exists when the personal viewpoints of TV station managers and vice-presidents interfere with our personal freedom of choice to watch or not to watch."

Phil was likewise enraged. And in a style reminiscent of the battles he used to have with WHIO management way back in Ohio, when he felt he had been censored, he did not keep his feelings to himself.

"The people who censor television are mostly men," he said, "and the whole issue of vaginal exposure emotionally paralyzes a lot of men. They are denying our viewers, who are mostly women, access to information which most women are more than ready to accept. The male attitudes toward women are especially apparent in daytime television, which is controlled by men. Daytime TV is almost all soap operas and game shows, and there's a notion that somehow women have to be protected from this type of show. It's a gross underestimation of the maturity of the audience."

Yet why should Phil Donahue be exempt from that group of men he claims control television? Why should he feel his show can better speak to women, or even *for* women, and understand their problems? It sounds a bit reminiscent of male gynecologists who consider themselves liberated because their patients address them by their first names, yet who blithely tell women what pains they should or should not be experiencing. For Phil Donahue is a man and one who admits now and then to a remnant of sexist response. What is it that makes his show strike such a sympathetic chord with a female audience?

The answer, in part, is Phil. Always sensitive to women, his experiences as a single parent—the hassles of shopping with teenage boys, the guilt of being a working parent—have given him the ability to relate to women in a way many other hosts cannot.

But a large part of the reason for his show's success in relating to women is that, except for a male director (Ron Weiner) and the executive producer (Richard Mincer), the Donahue staff is entirely composed of women. Pat McMillan, the woman who rose from being Donahue's secretary by having the nerve to speak up for herself (and by virtue of her abilities, of course) is producer of the show; she is backed up by two associate producers, Sheri Singer and Darlene Hayes (also with Phil since Cleveland). Press relations manager, station relations manager, production assistants, secretaries—they're all female, all reportedly very good.

And that matters. For, despite the impression any successful talk show gives of being a spontaneous affair—and the mistaken idea many viewers have that the talk-show host does all the research on his guests—the opposite is true.

Putting a talk show together takes an enormous amount of work, and almost nothing is left to chance. All major talk shows have researchers who delve into the backgrounds of the guests; producers who determine who the guests will be; writers who, often as not, put the questions into a host's mouth. (There is one popular afternoon talk-show host—the darling of the women's audience before Phil got so hot—who won't say hello unless it's written on a cue card.) The talk-show host who reads a guest author's book is very rare. Most often, the show's researcher has read the book, prepared questions, photocopied key passages, or—if there's a particularly relevant section—marks them for the host to read. (There's a New York talk-show host famed for his wit and erudition, who does an "intellectual" talk show— but when he interviewed Arthur Rubinstein, he did not read his guest's book; his researcher read it instead, and marked passages.)

Many guests on shows are "pre-interviewed"—that is, interviewed before appearing on the show in order to determine whether or not they'll be good conversationalists. Many are coached on what they can or cannot say. And a good producer or researcher will not simply get the background on a guest; he will—if he doesn't write out specific questions for the host—suggest *areas* of questioning: things that are of particular interest to whatever sort of audience they have. The insight and input of researchers, then, is critical. Surrounded by women staffers, Phil Donahue is not likely to miss the woman's viewpoint on a subject. He *is* likely to notice the dearth of women in high places elsewhere and—perhaps prompted by his staff, perhaps by his heightened awareness—confront Werner Erhard, founder of est, and ask him why more of his trainers are not women.

It's not just the host and guests that one must be careful with on a talk show, however; it's also the audience. A show doesn't just open up cold; someone always comes out to chat with the crowd, tell them what sort of questions to ask, point out the "applause" sign. Audience response is critical to the success of a television show; facing an indifferent audience, a performer on a show such as Carson's may freeze or perform badly. Carson's is the most successful talk show in the business, unbeatable in his slot. In that position, one might be considered popular enough to let audience warm-ups slide, but average warm-up before a Carson show takes ten minutes, with the show's producer, Doc Severinsen, and Ed McMahon taking part. Sometimes they get pretty bawdy in those warm-ups. In one recent warm-up, after Ed introduced Severinsen, the bandleader walked over to a piano and started making love to it.

"That'll give you a rough idea of where we're heading," said Ed. And later in the same warm-up, Ed announced that the drummer's wife had just given birth, and asked the proud father to take a bow—and the entire band rose in unison while the audience roared.

That level of tomfoolery does not quite take place before the Donahue show airs—though Phil will, in a pre-airtime hello to the audience, joke that his glasses make him look like a gynecologist, or pretend to sprinkle holy water on the crowd as he asks whether there are any Catholics there. And almost always, he makes that clever pitch: "Help me out, make me look good."

Audience warm-up is even more important, on a talk show like Phil's, than on Carson's—the audience, here, *is* the act. Also, with an hour to fill, and 240 shows a year to produce (plus Phil's eight-minute spots three times a week on the "Today" show), Donahue needs a sharp staff, a staff of self-starters who can come up with idea after idea. That the majority of the staff is female is the key to Phil's success—the reason his shows so often strike a chord with the audience—and Phil knows it.

"These women are to the show," he says, "what oil is to Saudi Arabia."

The head of this team—under the executive producer—is producer Pat McMillan, who contributes more ideas to the show than anyone else, and, by some accounts, has the greatest amount of clout in getting those ideas implemented.

"I don't have an absolute 'yes' on every subject I want," she says. "Still, if I really want it and can sell Phil, it will go. But it had better be good."

Her influence on the show is enormous. Besides providing a constant flow of program suggestions (Phil calls her a "human dynamo"), McMillan checks on props and lighting, and determines what sort of audience is best suited for a particular show. (For the show with Werner Erhard and a number of other self-improvement gurus, it was composed of graduates of those self-improvement programs; for a show with Masters and Johnson, and their book about homosexuality, it was an audience of gays.) McMillan also determines which members of the audience will sit closest to Phil, next to the stage, and thus be most often on camera. (The prettiest women are the ones most often selected.) Frequently, she does the warm-ups. (In the last moments of the warm-ups, Phil comes on and chats with the participants.)

As mentioned, those warm-ups are extremely important on the Donahue show. If women are nervous or intimidated, they won't ask questions. If someone makes them feel like hicks or novices or dummies, there's not a prayer that they'll speak up.

McMillan has the knack for making a roomful of women feel comfortable, and for making sure her show and its host look good, besides. She jokes, she teases—but she always advises them to shove their purses under their seats, keep their language clean, and not smoke or chew gum. "It looks awful on camera," she says. She warns them—nicely—not to be too frivolous. "Folks, if we hear one of you ask, 'How did you get your start in show business?' you'll see the entire staff throw up right here on the set." She encourages them to be expressive. "If you agree, or if you want to laugh, or if you want to go 'oohhh,' please do that out loud. If you want to boo and hiss, you can do that too. If you want to applaud, go ahead. Whatever you feel in your head, respond naturally."

Tall, blonde, slender, McMillan is also serious. She was offended by a reporter who described her as looking "like Farrah Fawcett-Majors' older sister." And she is also a feminist.

"I have a special commitment to women," she told *Ms.* magazine. "It's important to have women on the staff, because women still know more about what women want than men do. And our viewers want something besides fluff. Many shows I book are from the gut."

One of those shows was Phil's controversial program on abortion. McMillan was prompted to do that show by her own curiosity.

"I wondered what an abortion was like," she says. "So many people fear it. I found what I felt was the best abortion clinic in Chicago and did the show. I felt strange, watching. But I also felt it was our duty to put together a show that would allow a woman to make an intelligent decision at a time of great stress in her life."

Donahue respects her for her range of ideas—and for the fact that she keeps an eye out for *everything* on the show. She doesn't just line up a guest and leave the rest of it to the stagehands and engineers.

"She can put on a show that deals with sexual harassment in the office, and then she can also book a guy who does a striptease in a bar," Donahue says. "She has extraordinary insight. She can talk to the founder of a large chain of hotels and persuade him to appear. In the next breath, she can diagram where a combo of drums and bass should be on stage."

McMillan often says that she can understand the typical Donahue viewer because she *is* the typical Donahue viewer.

"In many ways, I'm her," she says. "I've been married, I've been through the humiliation of divorce court, I've worked, I've been confined to the home with nothing to do but watch game shows and soaps, I've had a mortgage, I've been thrown into the dating game after eleven years of being someone's wife . . . I feel as if I've been through a lot of the phases that the women who watch our show have been through."

She is also very much a self-made woman, who got her prestigious job not through connections, or even through a college communications course, but through hard work and competence.

"I grew up on a farm in Arcanum, Ohio," she told *Ms.* magazine. "Dayton was the nearest city. As a kid, my biggest ambition in life was to belong to the Book-of-the-Month Club. I finally saved enough of my allowance and joined. My parents taught me that if I really wanted to do something and tried hard enough, I'd succeed. My mother worked as manager of a plant cafeteria. I saw her as a strong person, with lots of class. My father had an intuitive sense of things."

Pat went to business school, worked briefly for United Airlines and, at an early age, married her high school sweetheart. She took a stint at full-time housewifery, but was bored within three months. ("I'm kind of a power person, controlling. I have to be important to somebody.") She got a job at WLWD in Dayton, working for program director George Resing. When "The Phil Donahue Show" started, McMillan became Phil's secretary, though being a secretary for the then-tiny show (there were only she, Phil, and Dick Mincer) included such offbeat tasks as picking up guests at the aiport. After hearing Gloria Steinem admonish women to speak up for the things they wanted, she spoke up for a job as a producer—and got it. Now she can be seen, when a show is in progress, standing to the side, taking notes, giving Phil discreet suggestions during breaks. Phil considers her invaluable.

"I'd have a real attack of insecurity if I looked up and she wasn't there," he says.

He also leans heavily on the other members of his behind-the-scenes team. Not a group of "yes-women," they criticize him if they feel he's gone for a glib joke rather than a serious follow-through, and refuse to buckle under if there's a show they really feel needs to be done.

One such show was on the subject of women and money. Phil was sure it would be a dreary bomb; his women staffers were convinced that women would love it. Phil finally concurred, and put on the show—and it's one of the most popular shows they've ever done.

"I can't get off a plane without someone thanking me for that show," says Phil.

Two other key members of Donahue's staff are his

associate producers Darlene Hayes and Sheri Singer.

Hayes, who has been with Phil since Ohio, planned a life as a housewife, not a career woman. But when she graduated high school (she's from Topeka), her mother gave her what Darlene now considers sage advice: "Take a year of business school, so if your marriage doesn't work out, you'll at least know how to type." When the marriage failed, and Darlene became a single parent of two, she signed on at the Donahue show. Like McMillan, she says she now often determines a show's content on the basis of her own curiosities and needs. "A lot of the shows I've produced have stemmed from frustrations in my own life."

Sheri didn't share many of those frustrations. At twenty-six, she is the youngest producer on the show, of another generation than Hayes and McMillan, and another lifestyle. The holder of a degree in radio-TV journalism, she has been a news writer and producer at several radio and TV stations. Precisely because she does represent a different generation—with another set of problems and attitudes—she is invaluable to Donahue. When Phil was doing a show on coed dorms, and wondered what it would be like if a girl came back to the dorm and found her boyfriend in bed with her roommate, he went straight to Singer, not to McMillan or Hayes. "I knew what it was like," says Sheri succinctly, "because it had happened to me."

The sort of tasks performed by Singer, McMillan, and Hayes—and the show's assorted assistants and secretaries—require diplomacy, fast response time, and a lot of horse sense. Of course, they're all always reading magazines and professional journals and newspapers, looking for ideas.

"We try to be on top of trends," Singer once told *TV Guide*. "Pregnancy is out, marijuana is out, breast cancer is getting that way. So are alcoholism and violence on TV and divorce, unless they are really something new. Stuff about babies is always good, that "erroneous zones" guy is good. Anything with marriage, couples, children. And sex. Sex always works. Always."

McMillan says, "The thing to learn is what is an issue *now;* Donahue can be *too* new with an issue. This farm-strike thing: Donahue said that it will only be an effective show when people can't get bread on the shelves. That's when we'll do it.

"There are shows that Phil doesn't do as well as others," she adds. "Vitamin therapy, biofeedback—he doesn't like those. And fashion and makeup shows. But he's learning. Before, all he could do was say how he hated blue eye shadow. Apparently he has this thing about blue eye shadow."

But often the women are required to do more than come up with ideas. A lesbian couple, scheduled to appear on the show with their kids, call the studio upset because their children's luggage has been lost. Phil's secretary and a production assistant are dispatched to buy the kids new clothes—by airtime.

Sammy Davis has a heart seizure minutes before his scheduled appearance, and McMillan is required, on the spur of the moment, to dream up a new topic for a show.

Of course, it is not entirely women who run the show backstage at "Donahue." Executive producer Dick Mincer has enormous power in determining what goes on at the show. So also does the show's director, Ron Weiner, who has won an Emmy for his work. Weiner watches the show from up in the control room, decides what faces in the audience will be televised, when to cut to Phil, when to the guest. As with everything else in the show, it's not left to chance. Ron knows exactly which faces to home in on: he tries to "mirror the people at home, the eighteen- to forty-nine-year-old housewife who's got some intelligence."

"I don't want them to look bored . . . don't want them to look ugly or too beautiful," he says.

Since women make up the bulk of Donahue's at-home viewers, Weiner zooms in mostly on women—with the rule never to photograph two men in a row. (Should Phil's demographics change, and more men start watching the show, which some people feel is happening, Weiner says he may be showing men more often.

But of course, whatever the skills of the people around him, a lot of the mood of the show is determined by Phil, who spends a great deal of energy on backstage activities, from warming up the audience, to joking with them through the breaks, to saying goodbye to them after each show.

A show he did with Margaret Trudeau, in front of a mammoth crowd at New York's Madison Square Garden (the Donahue show often visits other cities) was typical.

Pre-showtime, wearing open-necked shirt, sweater, and slacks, Phil was—in the words of one reporter— "combination PTA chairman, boy-next-door, and stand-up comic."

He had the audience—predominantly middle-aged women—shrieking with laughter as he described the sexist he had been in his married days.

"I drove home in my station wagon with the wood on the side, holding my alligator briefcase, wearing my white socks," he said.

He won the hearts of the crowd by letting them know that while he was liberal, he was not always *that* liberal. When a woman in the audience asked his opinion of lowering the drinking age, he came on like a responsible parent.

"Listen, I've got three kids with driving licenses in my house, and I hear the sirens every night. As a parent, I worry," he said.

He made a statement that endeared him to the women even more: "What I've come to realize is that while it's okay for a woman to get her man a beer, I wonder what reciprocal things he does for her . . ."

"Too many people are sleepwalking through life," he continues. "There are women here married to men who haven't kissed them in twenty years, or touched them, except in bed . . ."

The crowd erupts in applause. The women are convinced that this is a man who understands and appreciates them. Phil thanks them all for coming, says he has to go change, and turns the rest of the warm-up over to McMillan. Then, having changed into his trademark three-piece suit, he moves on the task of warming up his guest, Mrs. Trudeau.

"Be prepared for every question," he says, "and answer fast. Bring a sense of urgency to the show. Give me emotion."

The show begins. To communicate that sense of urgency, Donahue begins the show in his usual fashion, rushing into his introduction before the applause has died down, speeding through the first part of his talk as if someone may jump up at any moment and shoo him off the stage. And when it comes time for his discussion with Trudeau, he's done his homework well enough to pin her down when she waffles and doesn't answer a question to his satisfaction.

Trudeau's biography, *Beyond Reason,* does not paint a flattering picture of her husband, he says.

She disagrees. "I think it's a wonderful picture," she says.

"You mean writing about a country's leader who didn't talk to his wife, and gave her a black eye?" counters Donahue.

"Ah, maaaaan," says Trudeau.

"He treated you like a child, didn't he?" pursues Donahue.

"Yes, he did," she admits.

"He talked to you about nothing?" says Donahue.

"He talked about the children," she answers. "It wasn't the kind of marriage I'd dreamed of."

Later, Phil said goodbye to all the guests, just as he does after every show. But, while in Chicago, the goodbye—to two hundred women—need only take fifteen minutes or half an hour, in New York it went on for over an hour, with Phil clasping hands all the while, thanking the women for coming. "God bless you, glad you enjoyed it," he says.

His fans adore him, and many of his guests admire him, including Al Goldstein and Carl Bernstein, the reporter, who consider Phil the best interviewer they have ever come across.

Forty-three-year-old Al Goldstein is the publisher of *Screw*, the erotic tabloid now in its eleventh year of publication. Around New York, Goldstein is known never to be shy.

In recent years, Al has mellowed, but he's still someone who will generally say what he feels, on the air or off. He's also someone who has had his share of legal problems; at the time when he was a guest on Donahue's show, he had just been acquitted by a jury in Kansas of mailing pornography across state lines. (If found guilty of those charges, he could have gotten sixty years.) He is not likely to be greeted warmly by an audience of midwestern family people, for *Screw* is cheerfully, un-

ashamedly, enthusiastically a sexy, outrageous newspaper.

"I've done eleven years of television interviews, and
Phil is the best interviewer I've ever come across in
television," Goldstein says. "He does his homework,
he's enthusiastic, he's really a gentleman.

"To do television is to be exploitative. You get a
psychotic or a weirdo, and you put them on and your
TV ratings go up, and if you don't, they go down. But
if Donahue is exploiting, it's with sensitivity. I've never,
in all my years of television, seen someone edit out
something that was commercially to his advantage to
make a guest look good, but that's what Phil did to me."

Goldstein's gaffe, as he tells it, came at just about
the point during the show when the audience had decided
he was not such a bad guy after all, and as he and Phil
were taking questions.

"I was just turning the audience to my favor," says
Goldstein, "explaining how we're opposed to children
getting pornography, and how I wouldn't impose my
stuff on the unwilling, and how, anyway, pornography
does not lead to running out and raping a nun . . . at those
words—'raping a nun'—I lost them . . . during the next
break, Phil turned to me and said, 'Why'd you *say* that?
You had them!' I said, 'I don't know.' And later, he
edited it out of the show . . . I think he felt it had been
a disruptive and jarring remark . . . I'd never seen anyone
do that; if I interviewed someone for *Screw,* and they
called later to say they shouldn't have said what they
said, or really didn't mean it, I wouldn't have been so
honorable as Phil was to me . . ."

Goldstein also admired Donahue for other moments
during the show.

"At one point, he apologized to me after I told him

how none of the media had come to my defense during the federal indictment a few years ago. He said, 'I guess I have to take the blame for that, because I did not pay any attention to your plight, either.' And he wouldn't just let someone in the audience sit down after expressing animosity; he'd get them in a dialogue, say something like, 'What you're saying is that only *you* should allow what Americans can read?' There were a few times women seemed to feel I should be killed or burned. One woman said I was doing it for the money, and Donahue said, 'How come every time someone disagrees with somebody, they say they're doing what they're doing for money, but if they agree with them, it's an American success story?'"

Goldstein was equally as impressed with Phil when they were both off camera.

"I had five minutes with him before we went on," he says. "He was small-talking with me to calm me down ... they all do that in television ... my wife was with me, she loves him because of feminism and because of Marlo, and he was charming to her, and warm ... I still had no sense of him because TV moderators, as far as lasting qualities, are as insignificant as a McDonald's waitress—what really makes one different, from the next, y'know? He told me the audience would be angry at me, and I should work it to getting them to like me, and told me that I would gain nothing by being angry back. He said if they asked a hostile question, it would be because they were frightened. I felt like it was therapy, like I owed him a hundred dollars, like I was on the couch ..."

His respect for Donahue grew as the program progressed. And it was not diminished by Donahue's behavior after the show.

"We know most TV people are charlatans—that off

the air they're entirely different," says Goldstein. "But I actually got a sense that he respects the audience. I had booked a flight back to New York for right after the show, and he told me to cancel it. He wanted me to stay at the studio for an hour with him, and answer questions. He said to me, 'Some of these women have waited a year, two years; answer questions and meet them, you *owe* it to them.' To me, Phil Donahue is a very special person, he's a *mensch*. I'd do his show again on a moment's notice. I'm a fan."

CHAPTER TWELVE:

Happy All the Time

> I think everyone should have one of these. It's
> an education available at no university. You see
> a broader slice of life. I will never forget what
> has happened to me over the past ten years; I have
> changed personally, philosophically, in many,
> many ways...I'll never take this for granted."
>
> —Phil Donahue,
> "The David Susskind Show,"
> November 27, 1977

On a television talk show, late one Sunday night, not
very long ago, David Susskind played host, for an hour
and a half, to three of the country's most successful talk-
show stars: Dick Cavett, Stanley Siegel, and Phil Donahue.

The show touched on many things: the tensions of
running a show; the depressions that follow a bad show;
the philosophies of each host regarding how much of
himself to reveal; and what sort of things you should
never ask a guest.

At one point, Siegel got into a little spat with Donahue.

"I think we're all walking the thin line of ridicule up
there," Siegel began earnestly.

"No, no," said Phil, "that's the line they talk about with *you.*"

Yet with those little digs at one another, and with their questions to one another, the hosts all revealed their attitudes about what a good talk show should have. One of their biggest areas of disagreement was how to handle feelings. Stanley Siegel—whose show features himself lying on the couch in a five-minute session with an analyst—was the host who felt *all* should be revealed.

"I think talk shows should be *about* feelings," said Stanley. "We all have enough information; what we should do is say what we *feel,* and I'm willing to do that. Last December 31, I had no date, and it was New Year's Eve, and I laid on the couch and announced it. That's right, I had no date, unlike *you,* Phil . . . and after the show, Hal Prince [a New York director] called and said, 'You *must* come to my party.' My point is, I didn't do that just to be narcissistic, but to let people know that Stanley Siegel or someone on television is very much the way they are . . ."

"How will it make people at home feel any better when you say you don't have a date and get invited to Hal Prince's party, and when they say they don't have a date, they still end up staying home?" put in Cavett.

But Phil, later on in the show, voiced a different kind of concern about Stanley's approach—one that indicated that he thought the guest's feelings were just as important, and probably more so, than the host's.

"How do you evaluate your own ability to put the ball in the other guy's court? How do you evaluate your ability to help guests share the same honest feelings that you brag about feeling?" he asked.

It was, for all involved, a revealing show.

In asking David Susskind whether, after a bad show, did he "die a little—I mean, do you crash?" Donahue

revealed his own anxieties about producing a hit show.
He also revealed that he had been trying, in recent years,
to be a little easier on himself when he wasn't as sharp
or witty, during a show, as he had hoped to be.

"I think we overdevelop our own sense of responsibility," Phil said then, in reference to his long-ago stint
as a salesman. "I got out of this game several years ago,
because it was beating me up."

Now, he continued, he was trying to be more relaxed.

"We are not obliged to be walking encyclopedias,"
he said. "We are not obliged to have a nice, witty Don
Rickles/Dick Cavett stinger on the end of every segment
of the show. It's okay to scratch your head and say, 'I
can't think of any more questions.' That's really all
right ... What is this preoccupation in the talk-show
field with show business personalities? This parade of
talking heads who use words like 'marvelous,' and
'how long it took me to make my last movie' and 'my
marvelous album cover' and 'let me tell you about
what happened when we were shooting my last movie,
they were *wonderful* people, everybody on the movie
was a *family,* you could cut the love with a
knife' ... There's a feeling, especially in New York,
that because we're an entertainer, we're not going to be
interesting, and as we've all demonstrated, that is not
always true."

Phil restated his feeling that more talk shows should
use the audience.

"I came to Dick Cavett's show five or six years ago
with my son, and since he was underage, we were
obliged to sit in the balcony," said Donahue. "I felt very
disassociated from what was happening on the stage,
looking down through the proscenium arch, and I had
to look around the camera. I've never been able to understand why there is such a separation between the

talking heads and the audience . . . I wonder how really interesting any talking heads are going to be when we've got all that energy, all that feeling, all that talent out there. This is going to sound very self-serving, but why is it that no talk show involves and takes advantage of that talent and that energy which inconvenienced itself considerably to get here?"

Susskind replied that when his show had used an audience in the way Phil suggested, he had found it "counter-productive . . . the questions they asked were frivolous or off the subject." Siegel added—not unexpectedly—that what he thought was interesting in a show was the host's own life story.

Phil energetically disagreed.

"May I have your honest evaluation of this show?" he asked. When Siegel said he thought it was "fair," Phil continued, in characteristically blunt fashion, "I think it's a bomb, I think we're boring, I think the reviews are gonna say you could feel the egos, that four talk-show hosts got together and it was snoresville . . . I accept twenty-five percent of this bomb."

Actually, the *New York Times* reviewer said the show had been "crammed with interesting tidbits."

Phil also got into an altercation with Dick Cavett when he told Cavett that he disagreed with his approach when he told Timothy Leary, a guest on his show, that he was "full of crap."

"I really had a problem with that," said Phil. "I thought it was unnecessarily self-conscious for you to do that. I think you did that to get a response from the audience."

"I did," said Cavett, "but I incidentally thought he was full of crap."

"All right, but why did you bring him on the show?" asked Phil. "He said nothing that you didn't know, nothing that he hadn't already said . . ."

"You're not gonna give me that 'he was your guest and you owed it to him to be polite' business," said Cavett.

"No, if you think he's full of crap, then don't make him your guest, don't bring him on," said Phil.

"Oh, why not?" said Cavett angrily. "If a man has a wide influence and I think he's dangerous, then to have people see him and have someone point out that he's full of crap, for those too dumb to know, is a service."

At one point, Phil talked about how happy his show had made him.

"I think everybody should have one of these," he said. "I think it's an education available at no university . . . you see a broader slice of life . . . I go to lunch with Muhammad Ali, with Billy Graham, with atheists, with people running for president, with people going into jail, with people coming out of jail. I get a lot of attention, I get my name on TV. Every day, people ask me for my autograph. The money's good . . . I get a table at a restaurant . . . I will never forget what has happened to me over the past ten years . . . I've changed personally, philosophically, in many, many ways."

So he has. The man who was once an altar boy would angrily confront Father Andrew Greeley, a syndicated newspaper columnist and influential priest. ". . . you say, regarding the issue of sexuality, 'I don't know,' you sort of back away . . . I think you have an *obligation* to know . . ."

The man who once spent very little time with his children is now so involved with his kids that he can talk about them ceaselessly, before PTA meetings, with the women's magazines. "I'm home every night," he says. "And I touch them more. At least my kids know they are loved."

The man who was once indifferent to the feminist movement is now so passionate on the subject that he will even go after Rosalynn Carter, confronting her on the subject of why the President fired Bella Abzug as head of the White House National Advisory Committee.

"We needed someone who is quieter," said Mrs. Carter, in defending her husband's actions.

"But Mrs. Carter," objected Donahue, "that's what they said to Martin Luther King."

Granted, he is not a perfect feminist. On a program about dentistry, when he was taking questions, a woman in the audience spoke so knowledgeably that Donahue was impressed.

"You must be the wife of a dentist," he complimented her.

"I *am* a dentist," she replied.

On another show, he had an altercation with feminist Anne Gaylor, who had written a book on abortion. The book was pro-abortion, and Donahue's old streak of conservatism, and perhaps a bit of paternalism, was evident as he and Gaylor verbally slugged it out.

"Most people who appear on this program have their books held up," says Gaylor. "My book could not be held up because it is pro-abortion. Right?"

"No, that's not true," said Donahue. "I said I didn't want to show your book because I thought the title . . ."

"That the title was offensive to the Catholic Church," interrupted Gaylor.

"Okay, all right," said Donahue, visibly agitated. "Let me just tell you the title of the book. You're right, you're right. I asked you not to show the book. I engaged in a very blatant form of censorship."

"It was censorship," said Gaylor.

"The title is *Abortion is a Blessing*," said Phil. "I said that if you hold this book up, you're going to create such a shockwave that we're not going to get anything else done in here."

"I suggested we do it at the end of the program and you said no to that. Right?" pressed Gaylor.

"I thought that the title would be unnecessarily offensive to a lot of people," said Donahue. "That's what I mean. Why is it that you have to be so incendiary with your rhetoric?"

"Because I have conferred in over twelve thousand legal abortions, including a twelve-year-old girl, a fifteen-year-old . . ." said Gaylor. "I *know* abortion is a blessing. *You* won't let me say it."

"Okay . . ." began Donahue.

"Feminism has a long way to go on the Donahue show," said Gaylor furiously.

Would a serious feminist approve of the way, when Donahue visited Houston, a woman in her twenties posed for a picture with the interviewer, behaving like a star-struck teenager? "Give me a kiss," she said, "and my knees will go out." Would a serious feminist really appreciate the way Phil helps a woman to her feet during a show, or often holds her hand and gazes into her eyes when he asks a question? Would Dan Rather hold someone's hand as *he* asks her a question? Would Walter Cronkite? Would Morley Safer?

Would a serious feminist approve of the way Donahue sometimes treats his staff?

"He's overprotective of all of us to the point where he often treats us like children," producer McMillan told the *Chicago Tribune*, in an article entitled "The Women Behind Donahue." "When I was sick once, he had a woman from the station physically cart me off to a doctor I didn't want to see. He has this idea that he has to take care of us because he's the big daddy, but we're all adults here."

"There's a real streak of paternalism," added associate producer Singer. "He still feels he has to carry my bags at the airport."

There is also, the producers admit, a certain amount of irony involved in the fact that, while the show is sympathetic to feminists, the reality is that hundreds of women are waiting to see a *male* host.

"It's a real dichotomy," says Sheri Singer. "Here we are trying to explore feminism every day, but we still have these very traditional dynamics going on. We still have this chunk of women standing at the back of the studio every morning, waiting to talk to Phil. Yet what woman in the business has come across with that strong a personality?"

Adds associate producer Darlene Hayes, "We're still at the point where a lot of women won't go to a woman doctor. We've done shows on this. When we had some women priests on, there were a lot of women in the audience who felt very uneasy about it. I'm trying to think of the name of one woman who could do the show and be as effective as Phil is, and unfortunately I can't."

Phil is aware of the irony himself.

"There is nothing patronizing about my relationship with the audience," he says. "I do enjoy the company of women. But one of the revealing things that happens is that they ask me, 'How do you stand it with all these women?' I can see the self-loathing, the whole suggestion that women aren't interesting. When I hear things like that, I think of all the feminists who've been trying very hard to make the point about how our male-dominated culture smashes the spirit of women. It's hard to make that point. You get to where you sound like you want all women to run air hammers and fly airplanes and abandon their children. That isn't it at all. It is simply a matter of choices and relationships which include real choices for both men and women."

Just as he sees a certain self-loathing among some of
the women in his audience, he is also aware of the hos-
tility that many of the women feel toward the women's
movement.

"I still see a reluctance to identify with the movement,
and mostly from a woman who's married, two kids, mid-
thirties. A lot of them think that feminists are telling
them that if they got married when they were twenty-
two, had kids while the husband went off to work, drove
a station wagon with the wood on the side, and had a
split-level house in the suburbs, that after they've done
all that, the feminists are looking them in the eye and
saying, 'Baby, you've been had.'

"The important thing to remember is that feminists
haven't said that, but that's the way so many women
interpret them. What's interesting is the response, which
is usually anger. If that so angers you, then your anger
tells us more about you than you may want us to know."

As for his own ambivalence toward feminism, Phil
admits that there's a bit of the old sexist in him yet—
that, from time to time, he has wished that some nice
woman would make him breakfast in bed.

Still, unlike many men, Phil is aware of some of his
sexist leanings, and tries to work on them—and he feels
he's grown with women, with the members of his audience, and also with his staff.

"These are very proud women I'm dealing with, and
I've been affected by that pride, greatly," he says of his
production team. "I don't tell jokes here—'girl' jokes
or 'feminist' jokes. And while I don't mean that to sound
like a big concession, or suggest that I deserve a plaque,
I am saying that's the kind of understanding we have.
But this respect, this understanding is not something that
happened in a day. You don't go along in this culture

and get to be forty-three and suddenly get rid of all your sexism and prejudice. I didn't always treat women the way I do now."

Neither did he always live the way he does now.

For a romantic evening, he may drop over to the Consort Room at Chicago's Continental Plaza Hotel, and listen to Franz Bentler play schmaltzy old love songs on a hundred-thousand-dollar Stradivarius. Or he may go for a supper to Chez Paul, where, if he's late for the symphony, Chez Paul owner Bill Contos will insist he take the loan of his silver-and-blue Rolls-Royce, which was once owned by the Rolling Stones.

No, you need never wait, or be late, when you are a celebrity. Phil admits it himself; you go to the finest restaurants, get the best seats at the theater. If your girl lives in New York, while you live in Chicago, you can fly out on the spur of the moment to see her for the weekend. No need to consult your checkbook; the money is always there. If it's a bleak winter Thursday, and suddenly, from your office, you see that the snow is beginning to fall, you can take the kids and be off to Aspen the next day, after the show.

Insecurities about the show? With his new six-year contract, he can finally relax about that. And the way he's syndicated all over the country makes it hard to kill him off; you can die in Peoria and still be alive in Detroit. There's no one guy in charge of the entire act; no one guy who can say while he's shaving, "Donahue's getting soft; we can get another guy who doesn't have gray hair and has a larger vocabulary."

Insecurities about that gray hair? About his sex appeal, now that he's over forty? With a woman like Marlo Thomas as his wife?

As Margaret Trudeau would say, *"Ah, c'mon."*

* * *

It's an April evening in Chicago, and the half-a-million-dollar-a-year man is dressing. In a tuxedo, no less. Yeah, a tuxedo. Not tonight for the old jeans and sweater. Not tonight for a three-piece suit. Tuxedo time, now. Don't even have to rent them anymore. It's not the senior prom in Cleveland, that gray hair proves that. Not bad, though, that gray hair. Gives the old man sort of a dignified look. Elder statesman. No, elder talk-show host.

Big night tonight. Seven hundred people are going to pay $125 each to come to a dinner in his honor, to help him celebrate his show. Not that that's the official reason for the party. Gotta be accurate, gotta be an honest newsman, after all; the official reason everybody's coming to this party is a benefit for the Variety Club. Good group, the Variety Club, raising money for kids for . . . what is it? Fifty years now, something like that.

He's gotta move tonight. Marlo looks sensational in a white strapless dress; gotta get over to the Hyatt Regency. So many people coming by—the mayor, and Gloria, coming in from New York, and Billy Carter and Tom T. Hall and both Abigail van Buren and her sister, Ann Landers; Phil's mom would probably approve of that. Be fun to do a little partying tonight, after flying out to Vegas for that broadcast convention. And that May schedule—five shows in Detroit, shootings in West Virginia, and that set-up on the Mississippi Queen riverboat.

Arrive at the hotel. Blinding flashbulbs, TV crews, reporters. Like some old Hollywood premiere. Get in the middle of a bunch of those strobes, and it really does funny things to your eyes; you start seeing things there, for a minute.

There's F. Lee Bailey. There's Irv Kupcinet, who's

gonna emcee this shindig—will it be in his column tomorrow? There's Arthur Rubloff. Look at everybody
looking. Lot of them looking at Marlo. Lots different
than when Phil and Marge used to go out and they ignored her and were all over him, and when he had the
time, he'd see her putting on a nice front, and maybe
he'd have an attack of guilt. With a woman like Marlo,
it's something else entirely. Movie star, Danny Thomas's
kid—maybe more people want to see *her* than want to
see *him*.

Time for speeches. Gloria's up there on stage—watch
her charm them, bet she'll get a little politics in, though.
Sure enough.

"Phil is the only one that can get Marlo and me to
come to an unratified state," she says, in a reminder
about the ERA. A little praise, then: "Phil honors the
intelligence of the people who watch his show. Anyone
who watches daytime TV knows how rare that is." And:
"Phil has the most compassionate talk show on TV."
Then, back to politics, a suggestion that Mayor Bilandic
support the ERA. "I'm sure he is going to do this quickly
so we don't have to turn to Jane Byrne," she says.

More speeches. Ann Landers and Dear Abby are
gonna sing and dance. Silver dresses. Shimmy, shimmy.
A little bad blood, maybe, between those two—Ann,
introducing Abby as her "ugly sister"—was that *just* a
joke? Oh well, maybe so. They *are* a little off-key.
"Thank God they can write," says Irv, as they dance off.

Attorney F. Lee Bailey, taking the stage now, joking
that Phil is enormously successful because he heeded
Bailey's advice, to wit: "Try and conceal your lack of
intelligence. The American public is as dumb as you are
charming. Charm them."

Billy Carter's getting up there now, taking off his tie,
unbuttoning his shirt, saying that only his wife, Liz Tay-

lor, and Phil could get him into a tux.

Paul Anka's turn, singing Phil's praises to the tune of "My Way."

"There are no two/Like Donahue/Who interview/In such a whiz way," he croons. "He did it his way."

What would the guys back at the radio station at Notre Dame think if they could hear that? Or the guys at WHIO he used to battle with? The dream hits, and you have it all, all of a sudden, and even though you knew what it would be like, you didn't really know. Who ever knows? Who ever knows beforehand the smell of a limousine and how big it really is inside, or the feeling—when you are successful—of moving through an eternally cool, eternally air-conditioned universe? Who can ever imagine, beforehand, what it is like to have that almost invisible nod of the haughtiest maitre d' in New York, or to see the little flutter of excitement that comes over the stewardess as you get on the businessman's flight from New York to Chicago. You don't even have to tell them your name. They know it. "Welcome aboard, Mr. Donahue," they smile. And perhaps, with some, there will be that unspoken message that seems to continue after the hello smile: "And if you ever get tired of Marlo . . ."

Marlo—there she is now, onstage. That white dress, those bare shoulders. The band is playing "Danny Boy," her father's theme song. That's her little joke. Then Marlo, magic Marlo, is singing a song to him. A love song, new lyrics to that wonderful old standard, "A Fine Romance."

"We should go together/Like eggs and bacon
Except you always have to fly to Macon."

Beautiful. She's glowing. He's glowing. Everybody's looking at them. Everybody. Like a fantasy, like a Cleveland kid's fantasy, only better, better, 'cause who could imagine it this good?

He goes onstage.

He talks about Chicago: "I came here apprehensive; it's a big town with a lot of competition, and four years later, there is a nice big evening for me. If I'm not enjoying this, I should give it to somebody else."

He talks, with emotion, of Marlo: "She knows when I've died on my shows and when I've hit it. And she knows how to handle each occasion. She is what companionship is all about."

Smiles from the crowd. Applause. God, you can feel the audience, the love, the energy, the excitement. Like being onstage at Notre Dame, like doing a fine show. Oh, the good, powerful, loving audience.

"I shall never be the same," says Phil Donahue.